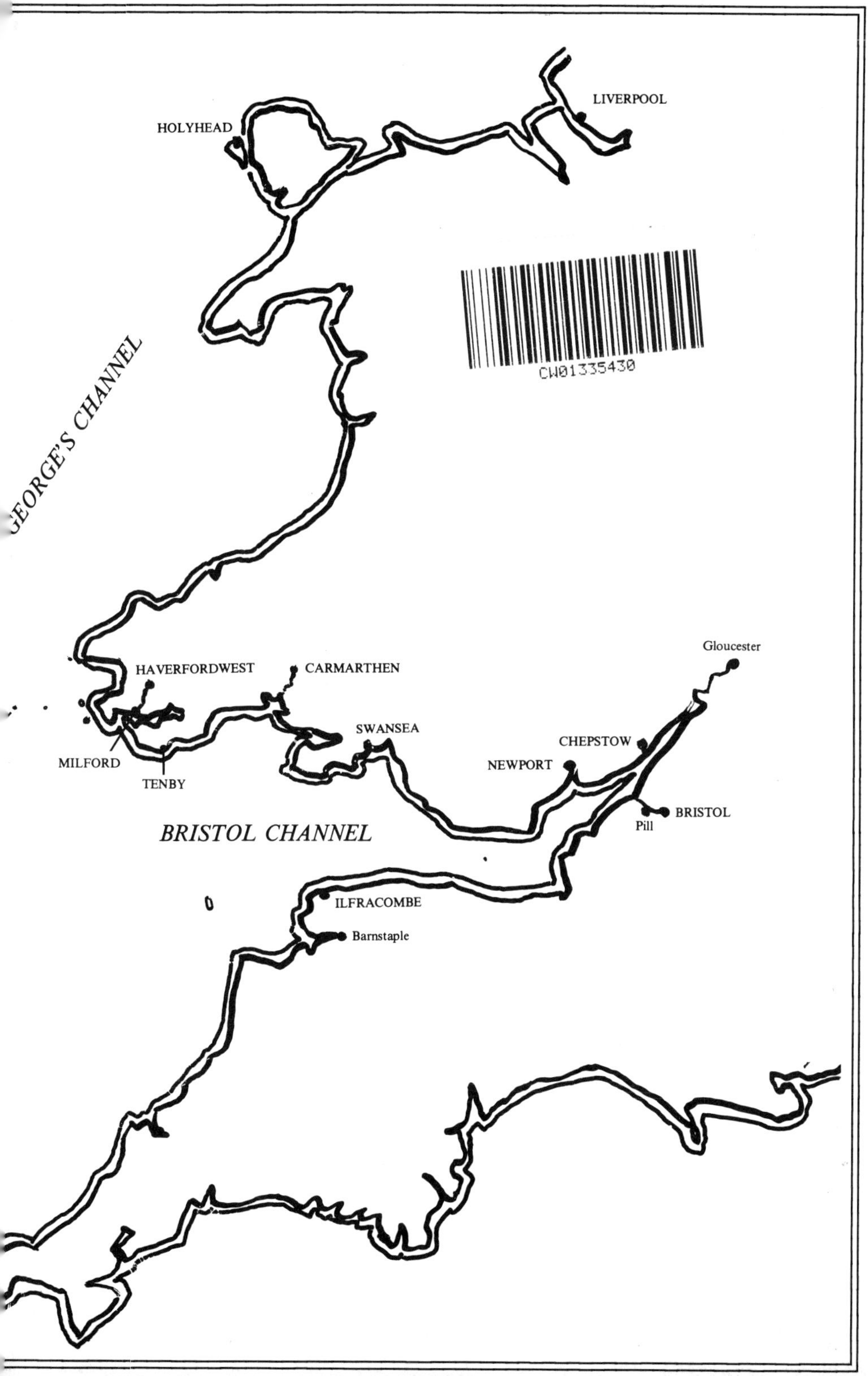

LIVERPOOL
HOLYHEAD
GEORGE'S CHANNEL
HAVERFORDWEST
CARMARTHEN
Gloucester
SWANSEA
CHEPSTOW
MILFORD
NEWPORT
TENBY
BRISTOL
Pill
BRISTOL CHANNEL
ILFRACOMBE
Barnstaple

EARLY BRISTOL PADDLE-STEAMER SHIPWRECKS

With an Introductory Sketch of the Beginning of Paddle-Steamer Activity out of Bristol

Merrivale of St. David's

Merrivale of St. David's
First published 1993
Copyright George Harries, 1993
ISBN 0 9515207 3 3

Photoset and Printed in Great Britain by
The Longdunn Press Ltd, Bristol

Contents

List of maps and illustrations	4
Acknowledgements	6
Introduction and Background	7
1. The *Frolic*, (1831)	34
2. The *Albion*, (1837)	45
3. The *Killarney*, (1838)	53
4. The *City of Bristol*, (1840)	76
5. The *Queen*, (1843)	86
6. Matters Arising	97
Glossary	105
Bibliography	107

List of Maps and Illustrations

Maps:

1. The Bristol Channel and Southern Ireland (inside front cover)
2. Milford Haven: showing also the islands of Skomer and Skokholm
3. Nash Sands
4. Jack Sound
5. Cork and the coastline around
6. The Rennies
7. Rhossili Bay
8. Bristol c.1820 based on *Donne's New and Correct Plan of Bristol, Clifton and the Hotwells* (by kind permission of Bristol Reference Library) (inside back cover)

Illustrations:

Cover: *A steamer on the River Avon passing Pill, c.1835*

1. *S.P. Glamorgan entering Swansea Harbour*
2. S.P. Glamorgan advertisement
3. *The Gloucester House and Steam Packet Hotel*
4. *S.P. Lady Rodney* advertisement
5. *S.P. Palmerston* and *George IV* advertisement
6. *S.P. Hibernia* and *St. Patrick* advertisement
7. *The Duke of Beaufort passing Rownham Ferry, Hotwells*
8. Timetable of the Bristol & Chepstow Steam Packet *Duke of Beaufort*
9. *S.P. Duke of Beaufort* advertisement

10. *The Avon Gorge at Sunset*
11. *Nash Sands Lighthouses*
12. Model of Paddle-Steamer: photograph
13. Wreck of the *Albion*: photograph
14. *The wreck of the steamer* Killarney *of Bristol on a rock at Renny Bay co. Cork*
15. *Captain Manby's mortar lifeline*
16. *The wreck of the steamer* Killarney *of Bristol . . . showing the scene of the disaster . . . & the mode of rescue*
17. Wreck of the *City of Bristol*: photograph
18. *Portrait of Baron Spolasco*
19. Baron Spolasco advertisement

Acknowledgements

No one who knows the late Grahame Farr's work on Bristol ships in the 19th Century, and on West Country passenger paddle-steamers in particular, will be surprised to see his name at the head of the list.

I readily acknowledge my debt to his work.

I wish to thank the staff of Bristol Reference Library; Francis Greenacre of Bristol City Museum and Art Gallery; Andy King of Bristol Industrial Museum; staff of Bristol Record Office; the Departments of Manuscripts and of Maps and Prints of the National Library of Wales at Aberystwyth; Lloyd's of London; Joan Evans, former reference librarian at Haverfordwest Library; Clive Hughes of Haverfordwest Record Office; West Glamorgan County Library, Swansea; Deidre Hamill of Trinity College Library, Dublin; Mary O'Doherty of the Library, Royal College of Surgeons of Ireland; the National Army Museum; Kieran Burke of Cork City Library; J. C. Robinson of the Science Museum, South Kensington; staff of the National Maritime Museum; the Guildhall Library, Aldermanbury; Anne Rainsbury of Chepstow Museum; staff of Chepstow Library; and Ray Davies of the Glyn Vivian Art Gallery, Swansea.

Of individuals, I am grateful to the following for their help: Nathan Illston, formerly Officer of Nash Point Lighthouse; Marcus Morris; Nick Georgano; John Wilson-Smith; Robin Craig; Meurig Harries; H. J. Dickman; Jeffrey Spittal; Roger Heath; Charlotte May; Patrick Hickman Robertson; Gerald McSweeney; Ben Harries for doing the maps; Judith Maxwell for generous help especially on matters nautical; and to Peter Davies for much encouragement and sound advice.

George Harries

The quotations from the Diary of Lewis Weston Dillwyn and the manuscript of a journey made by Sir Richard Colt Hoare are made with permission of the National Library of Wales.

Introductory Sketch of the Beginnings of Paddle-Steamer Activity out of Bristol

The stories of the five shipwrecks told here are complete in themselves. However, they are also but episodes in a much longer story of continuing enterprise and activity.

In order to strike some sort of balance it might help to sketch in something of that background story.

For this purpose a look at the doings of paddle-steamers sailing regularly in and out of Bristol in the year 1823 would seem to be most suitable. For that was the year in which the paddle-steamer first established a pattern of packet services from Bristol to destinations within the Bristol Channel and across in Southern Ireland that remained recognisable, for the most part, 50 years or so later.

It was the coming of the railways that spelt the end of the hey-day of Bristol's paddle-steamer packets.

Nevertheless, 1823 was the year when the steam packet services out of Bristol, as Grahame Farr put it, 'passed out of the era of experiment'.

But first, a look back at the time of the sailing packets before steam came to Bristol. Within Bristol docks you would see, apart from the great ocean-going ships and Irish sailing packets, numerous small vessels from ports and inlets along the coasts of Somerset, Devon, Cornwall and Wales; many with humble names like *Betsey* or *Flora*, *Lucy* or *Lydia*, *Mary*, *Eliza* or *Jane*.

On the Welsh Back there would be those from Chepstow, Newport and Caerleon with farm produce, capons, geese and pig to roast on the spit, butter and cheese, and fruit in season to sell at the market there. Prices went up in Bristol when bad weather prevented their coming. They came in on Wednesdays and they went out on Thursdays. You could go with them if you liked. It would cost you a shilling to Newport, and could take up to 12 hours, for they used the tide; though it would take much less if the wind were favourable.

They were sloops, these market boats. They were decked to

protect the produce, and there was a cabin for the passengers. The *Chepstow*, for example, was a substantial vessel registered at 69 tons with a length of 54 ft., and she was capable of carrying about 60 passengers at a pinch.

Others from along the South Wales coast made their way to Bristol, carrying whatever goods they had to sell, mainly produce from the farm. They functioned as goods vehicles at a time when for many places the sea gave better access than the roads.

From Pembrokeshire and Cardiganshire in the far west there came yet more sloops, single-masted, of course, and ranging from less than 20 tons burthen to 40 tons or so; some one man and a boy affairs, carrying corn preferably in sacks, butter and cheese; and with orders and shopping by commission, and favours to do. Groceries, haberdashery and ironmongery for the shopkeeper perhaps; and take what comes for cargo. Like the boiler, oven and grate, with a roll of carpeting bought by the Rev. David Griffiths, vicar of Nevern, near Newport in Pembrokeshire, on a visit to Bristol in 1802: yet more carpeting and other things for his wife's parents Mr. and Mrs. Bowen of nearby Llwyngwair, all of it shipped on board the *Maria*, Capt. Davies, Cardigan; though Mr. Griffiths, himself, and his wife took the mail coach to Narberth, where they were met by servants with horses to take them home.

Still in Pembrokeshire, a few miles to the north-east of St. David's, the tiny inlet of Abercastle, like others along the coast, kept in intermittent touch with Bristol.

And it was sloops from Abercastle like the *Ann and Mary* of 17 tons burthen, the *Cambria* and the *Eagle*, for example, that Peter Williams, a corn-factor in Bristol, about 200 years ago, used to help keep in touch with his nephew John, a farmer at the family home at Trearched, in the nearby parish of Llanrhian. He sent letters by them sometimes instead of using the mail. Once there was a basket of apples for Mrs. Williams and the children at Trearched; again, this time in the *Cambria*, Capt. James James, a load of paving stones for the hall and passage of the farmhouse there, already jointed, faced, and numbered on the back, ready to be laid according to a plan. Another time it was ten winchesters of wheat seed sent in two new sacks; then it was some old furze seed, now more usually called gorse, to grow on to make hedges for shelter.

In fact such vessels having delivered their corn and butter to Bristol returned with whatever was required, anything from furniture to pins, not forgetting seed for the farmer, and all of it transacted on a personal level.

They had their own pace those Pembrokeshire sloops. The *Dove*, Joseph Jermyne, of Tenby or the *Active*, William Williams, of Haverfordwest, for example, after arriving at Bristol, might take about a fortnight for unloading and loading. You would find them at the Second Ladder on the Welsh Back. Sailing for home, they would be back again in three weeks, sometimes less than that in the summer, more in the winter. Where they did 8 or 9 voyages, the *Milford Packet* and *Liberty*, 38 tons burthen, both of Haverfordwest, might do 4 or 5 in the time.

Passengers were those, who rather than go by coach, were prepared to take the risk. It might be the antiquarian, who was so carried away in St. Brides Bay by the sight of the Bishop and his Clerks off Ramsey Island that to him they appeared, 'like so many heads of gaping monsters ready to devour, watching as fancied dragons, with gaping mouths, fiery hissing tongues, and snorting iron snouts.' Or it might be a schoolboy, like Samuel Williams of St. David's, less enthusiastically making his way in his father's *Favourite Nancy*, under the care of John Rees, to Mr. George Pocock's Prospect Place Academy on St. Michael's Hill in Bristol.

From harbours and inlets and up-river ports they came, many long since disused. From Langport, Minehead and Porlock, Barnstaple and Bideford, Boscastle and Hayle, from Aberthaw, Carmarthen, Laugharne, Solva and Abercastle and places like them, small vessels came and went on business inspired by Bristol, unhurried and in the habit of waiting until the wind 'served'.

For travellers going to Ireland, on the other hand, the whole basis of their journey was different. They had no choice; the last stage had to be a sea voyage, be it from Bristol, Milford Haven, Holyhead, Liverpool or elsewhere.

Before the introduction of steamers, there were 14 sailing vessels advertised on the War Office and Commercial Packet list as maintaining a packet service between Bristol and Southern Ireland. As packets, this meant, in effect, they would carry passengers and general goods according to a regular programme. The livestock imported from Ireland travelled in separate vessels.

Three vessels were set aside to provide a weekly service to Dublin; eight to cover the twice weekly service to Cork; and three more to serve Waterford three times a month. Under sail a passage from Bristol to Cork or Dublin of three days or so would be very satisfactory.

These sailing packets were not large compared with the West

Indiamen many of which were 300 or 400, and a few even 500 tons*. Indeed, of the two newest, the *Express Packet*, a cutter, was 61 tons, and the *Earl of Moira*, a sloop, was 51 tons.

No doubt passengers had stories to tell about their crossings. Samuel Carter Hall, enjoyed telling his, remembering the detail and the flavour years later.

After embarking at Bristol, it was, he claimed, six weeks before he arrived at Cork:

> The packet could not sail in the teeth of a foul wind, or, after starting, had to give in and wait for a change . . .
> The accommodation on board was wretched: there was no woman-steward; the berths for women were never separated from those of men – even by a screen . . . To undress was out of the question . . .
> Each passenger took his own sea store. Salt junk and hard biscuit were the only food to be obtained if the voyage lasted above three or four days . . .
> Often the "sea-stores" ran short before half the voyage was over; and between contrary winds, miserable accommodation, and the scarcity and bad quality of provisions, a passage to Ireland was often a more serious and expensive undertaking than now a voyage to New York.

He was writing about 50 years after the event. 'Putting out and putting back,' was worrying, 'but nobody dared risk the sleeping ashore.' Certainly not Samuel Carter Hall, a schoolboy then, going home to Ireland for the holidays in the year of Waterloo.

At that time, 1815, the paddle-steamer, proving itself on the Clyde, was soon to show its paces on the Mersey and the Thames. At Bristol, however, the management structure was too cumbersome to handle effectively the problems and opportunities that were coming its way. Whereas Liverpool, like Bristol with Irish and transatlantic interests, was in expansive mood.

In 1821, at last a group of Bristol merchants committed themselves to steam by placing orders for two paddle-steamers, the *George IV* and the *Palmerston* with Messrs. Hilhouse at their yard in Bristol. At the same time a Liverpool based company was also planning to run steamers to Ireland out of Bristol.

* To avoid confusion 'tons' when used by itself refers to the registered tonnage of a vessel.

The Bristol merchants were encouraged by the War Office, which decided to abandon using sailing packets and change over to steam. It advertised a contract to provide a weekly service from Bristol to Cork and to Dublin for transporting by steamer soldiers, recruits and convicts to and from Ireland, thus renewing its confidence in Bristol as a port of transit.

Changing over to steam was a big undertaking, and the merchants on winning the contract signalled their success by calling themselves the War Office Steam Packet Company. The contract gave them an important nucleus of business. There were large numbers of troops garrisoned in a restless Ireland from Napoleonic times for the rest of the 19th Century. To give actual figures, in 1828, for example, of 30,000 British infantry in the United Kingdom, 25,000 of them were either stationed in Ireland or strategically placed on the west side of the mainland ready to be moved there. No doubt the company felt its official recognition by the War Office would make its ships more attractive to government officials generally, the clergy of the ecclesiastical establishment, as well as the nobility and gentry with estates in Ireland.

In 1822 much was learnt about the operation of steamers in Bristol. The first steamer packet services had been set up. There was one to Liverpool via Dublin, one to Cork, another to Chepstow daily, and two rival daily services to Newport.

It was the Liverpool based St. George Steam Packet Company which provided the pace with the *St. Patrick* and the *St. George*, each it was claimed of 300 tons burthen. On the other hand, the War Office Company made a disastrous start. The *George IV*, 126 tons, had to give up after a few weeks, her engines were not up to it: the *Palmerston*, 115 tons, failed to appear at all.

Despite those particular difficulties, however, by 1823 the capacity of the paddle-steamer to operate in the specific conditions of the Bristol Channel and the Irish Sea had been proved beyond reasonable doubt. Of course there were still small difficulties, but people were not unused to them; like, for example, Lewis Weston Dillwyn of Penllergaer, delayed at Bristol, who noted in his diary: 'I had intended to have gone by the Steam Vessel to Swansea, but she did not arrive in her usual course. Spent the day geologically.'

Bristol was seeing for itself the advantages of steam over sail. Steamers could sail to a timetable without having to wait for the favour of the wind before setting out. Furthermore, the steamer was proving to be particularly suitable for short passages like the one to Ireland where there was no need to refuel *en route*.

From the owners' point of view there were disadvantages. Valuable freight space was taken up by the engine and its coal supplies. Equally importantly, a steamer consumed large quantities of coal, and therefore was expensive to run.

This is not the place to go into the technicalities of early marine steam engines, but one or two statistics might be illuminating, despite the confusing use of m.p.h.. Statistics of this kind are difficult to find and these particular ones concern two Clyde steamers from John Scott's yard at Greenock. The *Superb* built in 1820, 240 tons with engines of 72 nominal h.p., in trials used about ¾ ton of Scotch coal per hour at 9 m.p.h.. To build she cost about £37 a ton gross. The *Majestic*, built in 1821 and larger at 345 tons, with engines of 100 nominal h.p., steaming at 10 m.p.h. used 1 ton of Scotch coal per hour. And she cost over £40 a ton gross to build.

A steamer, by rule of thumb, cost about three times per ton gross more than a sailing packet to build. Ships like the *Killarney*, *Albion* and *Queen*, it seems, would have cost somewhere between £15,000–£20,000. Thus they had to be kept busy to bring in a reasonable return.

Any sketch of paddle steamer activity in the season of 1823 must convey the novelty and excitement of it all. Companies made bright claims for their ships and the services they offered. In the days of sail you just took what was going. In 1823 the companies were reaching out to tempt you.

1. *S.P. Glamorgan entering Swansea Harbour*: aquatint, c.1830 (by kind permission of the glyn Vivian Art Gallery, Swansea City Council Leisure Services Department).

For the Swansea packet the *Glamorgan*, 59 tons, for example, it was claimed she provided:

> The most comfortable, cheap and expeditious Travelling between BRISTOL, CLIFTON, CARDIFF & SWANSEA: forming the most direct communication between South Wales, Bristol, Bath, Cheltenham, London, Oxford, Birmingham, and all parts of the North. . . . Travellers from the South of Ireland will find great advantage in availing themselves of this conveyance as several Coaches are established between Milford and Swansea, thereby avoiding the inconvenience and delay often experienced in crossing at the Old and New Passages. . . . No expense has been spared in making her accommodation as elegant and commodious as possible; and she is provided with a Female Steward to attend the Ladies.

The *Duke of Beaufort*, 58 tons, the Chepstow packet, had been 'newly painted and equipped for the Season . . . will continue to ply daily . . . no exertion shall be spared to render every possible Accommodation to Passengers.'

Lady Rodney, also 58 tons, a Newport packet for many years, '. . . built expressly for the Station . . . a beautiful and very superior Vessel of her class . . . she has a double Engine of the power of 28 Horses.'

A eulogy of the *George IV* in the Cork Morning Post says she is:

> . . . celebrated for the celerity and punctuality of her voyages . . . the elegance as well as the convenience with which she is fitted up, having distinct and separate compartments for Ladies and Gentlemen. . . . The foul smell, which contributes so much to render the passenger sick in ordinary vessels, cannot exist in this, a most desirable effect, produced by no paint being used in the cabin and sleeping apartments, which are laid with mahogany and by the vessel making no water in her hold. . . . A trip to Bristol now is . . . a few hours. The traveller from any part of the South of Ireland finds himself in the West of England, within 12 hours' journey of London, without a toilsome land journey to exhaust his spirits . . .

On a more mundane level, it has to be said that a traveller taking the London Mail coach from the Bush tavern in Corn Street would reach Piccadilly 120 miles and 14 hours later; others took longer.

Just as at Cork crowds of people flocked to see the *George IV*

BRISTOL and GLAMORGAN STEAM-PACKET COMPANY.

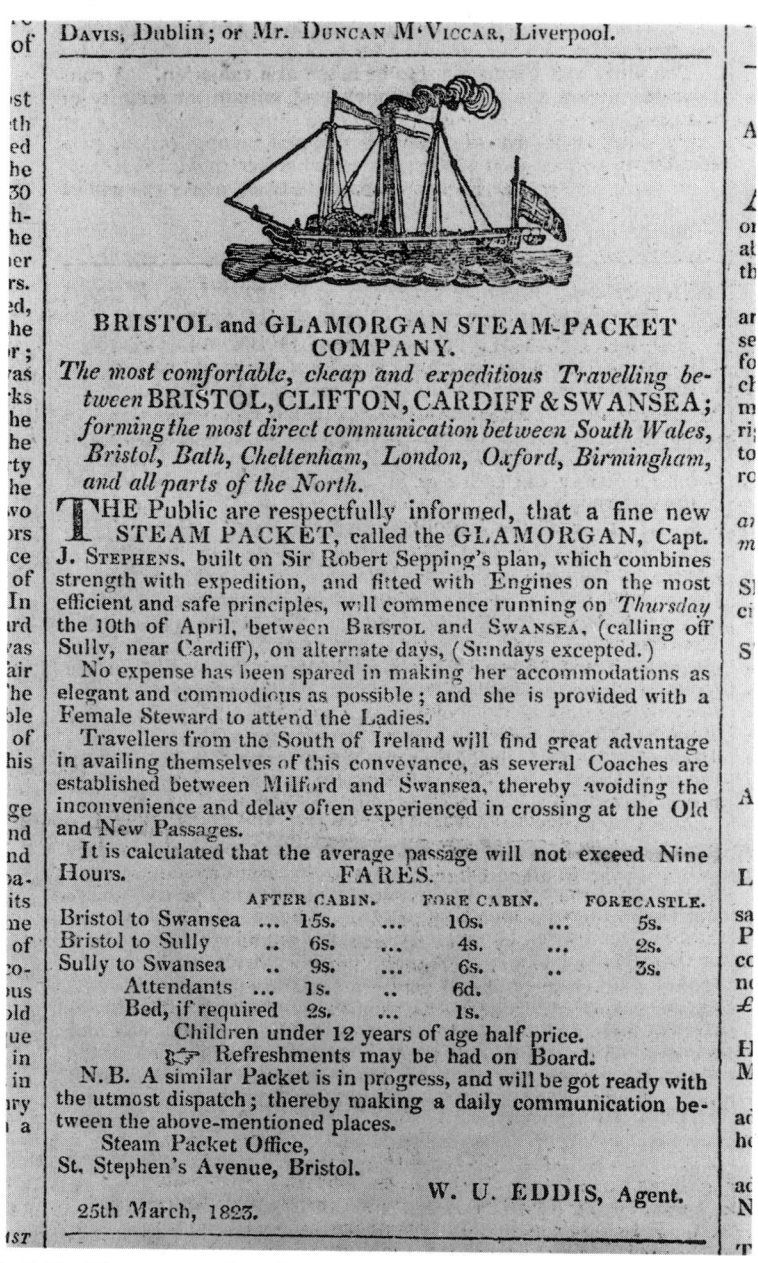

The most comfortable, cheap and expeditious Travelling between BRISTOL, CLIFTON, CARDIFF & SWANSEA; *forming the most direct communication between South Wales, Bristol, Bath, Cheltenham, London, Oxford, Birmingham, and all parts of the North.*

THE Public are respectfully informed, that a fine new STEAM PACKET, called the GLAMORGAN, Capt. J. STEPHENS, built on Sir Robert Sepping's plan, which combines strength with expedition, and fitted with Engines on the most efficient and safe principles, will commence running on *Thursday* the 10th of April, between BRISTOL and SWANSEA, (calling off Sully, near Cardiff), on alternate days, (Sundays excepted.)

No expense has been spared in making her accommodations as elegant and commodious as possible; and she is provided with a Female Steward to attend the Ladies.

Travellers from the South of Ireland will find great advantage in availing themselves of this conveyance, as several Coaches are established between Milford and Swansea, thereby avoiding the inconvenience and delay often experienced in crossing at the Old and New Passages.

It is calculated that the average passage will not exceed Nine Hours.

FARES.

	AFTER CABIN.	FORE CABIN.	FORECASTLE.
Bristol to Swansea	15s.	10s.	5s.
Bristol to Sully	6s.	4s.	2s.
Sully to Swansea	9s.	6s.	3s.
Attendants	1s.	6d.	
Bed, if required	2s.	1s.	

Children under 12 years of age half price.

☞ Refreshments may be had on Board.

N.B. A similar Packet is in progress, and will be got ready with the utmost dispatch; thereby making a daily communication between the above-mentioned places.

Steam Packet Office,
St. Stephen's Avenue, Bristol.

W. U. EDDIS, Agent.

25th March, 1823.

2. *S.P. Glamorgan* advertisement: Felix Farley's Bristol Journal (by kind permission of the Bristol Reference Library).

when she was in harbour, so the *Hibernia*, 245 tons, of the St. Patrick Steam Packet Company attracted considerable attention when she made her long awaited appearance in Bristol. She was thrown open to visitors for a whole day 'to the manifest injury of her elegant carpets and floor-cloths.'

A press report pronounced her to be 'an immense Floating Hotel, equal in all her equipments to the York House or Clarendon Hotel . . .' After remarking that 'her mirrors and mahogany pannels far surpass those of the *Royal Sovereign* . . .' and being prevented by the crowds from listing her 'peculiar excellencies', the report continued:

> but we were so delighted and surprized with the novel and refreshing sight of her commodious Lavatory, furnished with cisterns, immense basons, ample light, and large mirrors, where all who have been afflicted with sea sickness, may purify themselves from its disagreeable effects previous to their landing, that we cannot refrain from adverting to this most important article of comfort, and which to an Englishman lays the foundation of all his other enjoyments.'

Despite the novelty of it all a routine was being established. The steam packets found their own place among the West Indiamen, emigrant ships for New York or Quebec, traders bound for the Baltic, the Black Sea, and the Mediterranean; among the ships, barques, brigantines, snows, and coastwise schooners, smacks and sloops, and trows from the Severn and Wye.

In 1823 the War Office Company with its offices at 1, Quay, near the Drawbridge, in the very heart of Bristol, had the *Palmerston* going to Dublin once a week, and the *George IV* to Cork, both from Cumberland Basin, Hotwells. The Company also had the *St. David*, 56 tons, sailing from Cumberland Basin to and from Newport daily, and the *Cambria*, 48 tons, from Bathurst Basin, near Queen Square. *The Cambria* started the season going also to Newport, but before the end she was going to Chepstow and taking on passengers at Cumberland Basin on the way.

Close by the company's offices on the Quay, the proprietors of the Nelson tavern, opposite the Drawbridge, were caught up in the new excitement for steamships. They decided that Nelson had had his day, and his tavern became the Steam Packet Hotel, *sic transit gloria mundi*.

Not surprisingly this idea caught on in Hotwells, which was

3. *The Gloucester House and Steam Packet Hotel*: J. Price, c.1823 (courtesy of Bristol Museums & Art Gallery). The hotel was refurbished and re-named especially to attract steamer passengers.

well placed for passengers off the packets and where the macabre business of 'taking the waters' was in decline. There the large premises of Gloucester House with its attendant Gloucester Inn near Cumberland Basin was given a new lease of life by George Warne when he restyled it the 'Gloucester House and Steam Packet Hotel'.

Conveniently the St. Patrick Steam Packet Company had its offices in Gloucester House. From there it organised the *St. Patrick* and the *Hibernia* to go to Dublin once a week. The *Hibernia* was dogged with problems. And the failure of the *Hibernia* gave the *St. Patrick* the chance to show its capacity. Soon it was being reported that the *St. Patrick* had completed passages from Bristol to Dublin, Dublin to Bristol, and then back again to Dublin all in the space of six days.

Operating from offices in St. Stephen's Avenue, the Bristol and Glamorgan Steam Packet Company started the season with the

Glamorgan, which after a few weeks was joined by the *Bristol.* They too sailed from Cumberland Basin. After experimenting with a return trip between Ilfracombe and Swansea twice a week, the final schedule was: Bristol to Tenby every Monday; Tenby to Bristol on Tuesdays; Bristol to Ilfracombe on Wednesdays and Fridays, returning on Thursdays and Saturdays; that was for one vessel. The other, not to be outdone, plied between Bristol and Swansea on Mondays, Wednesdays and Fridays and returned to Bristol on Tuesdays, Thursdays and Saturdays. It was calculated the average passage for this would not exceed 9 hours.

Perhaps it is worth noting here that the Cambrian coach, travelling at a more leisurely pace than the Mail, leaving from the Bush tavern in Corn Street took 16 hours over the 82 miles to Swansea, with the fearful Severn to be crossed on the way in an open boat.

J. and W. Jones operated the *Lady Rodney*, which left for Newport daily, taking about $3\frac{1}{2}$ hours and returning the same

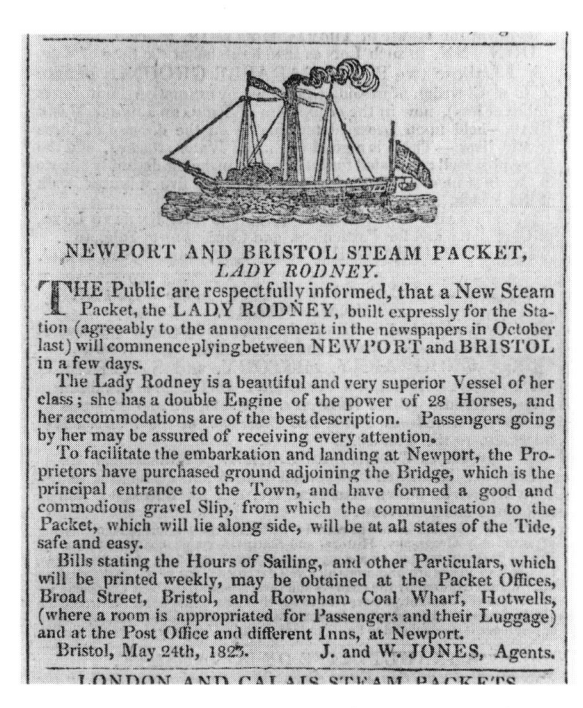

4. *S.P. Lady Rodney* advertisement: Felix Farley's Bristol Journal (by kind permission of the Bristol Reference Library).

day. They also sent the *Duke of Beaufort* to Chepstow daily. Both went from Rownham Coal Wharf at Hotwells, where the agents had an office and there was a room for the passengers' luggage so that they could avoid the pressing attentions of the porters there, who were much complained of.

In these early days much was learnt by trial and error. Routes had to be tested to discover demand, and the steamers tested for their suitability for their tasks. For example, the War Office Company stated in March that its *Duke of Lancaster*, 95 tons, would try out a service between Bristol, Ilfracombe and Tenby; during May she was advertised to sail from Bristol to Dublin, calling at Tenby; in September she was leaving Cumberland Basin every Tuesday for Waterford. Six months later she was offered for sale.

Before considering fares, a brief look at the value of goods and services in 1823 might help to provide a rough standard for comparison.

For example, the commonest wage for a farm labourer in the West Country was, it seems, 7s. a week. He would have a cottage and some produce as well.

A widow with two small children in a Somerset mining village, with rent already paid, received 4s.6d poor relief.

Round about this time a "hobbler", rowing a tow-boat on the Avon, would make on average about 7s.6d. a week.

Poor young girls in Bristol working at home could earn between 2s. and 3s. a week putting heads on pins for Messrs. Croucher & Kirby of Gloucester, Pin Manufacturers, at 4d. per lb..

The going rate for the cheapest kind of housing in the parish of Castle Precincts, not the poorest parish in Bristol, a tenement in Rouch's Court or Sheppard's Court in Queen Street, say, was £3 per year. There was some accommodation at £2 10s. in the parish, but it was scarce.

In the country the meanest village cottage would have a rent of 1s. a week.

Coal prices varied. But, for example, 27 tons delivered to the Poor House at Westbury on Trym during the year ending March 31, 1823 cost 16s.4d. a ton. It seems that this was good quality coal. Coal prices varied about 4s. a ton according to quality.

For a time in 1823 beef and mutton were selling for 4d. to 5d. per lb. in Bristol Cattlemarket, and pork at 3d. to 3½d..

In Bristol the average price for a quartern loaf of bread, somewhat over 4lbs., was 8¼d.; during the year it varied between 6¾d. and 9½d. The price of bread was crucial to the poor and a rise in price meant even more hardship.

Newspapers were a luxury. The Bristol newspapers, published weekly, cost 7d.. As they put it, 'tax 4d., paper & print 3d.' A cheaper way to read the news was pay a subscription to a reading room.

The rector of Upper Slaughter thought an annual rent of about 13s. an acre low for his rectorial farm of just over 200 acres.

For the rich there were opportunities. At the picture sale at Fonthill, A Portrait of Sir Thomas More by Hans Holbein went for 100 guineas, 'The Infant Saviour' by Leonardo Da Vinci fetched £105, which amounted to the same thing.

Everybody complained that times were hard, but for the poor there was no leeway.

With regard to fares, in 1823 you could go to Swansea or Ilfracombe for 16s. in the after cabin, 10s.6d. in the fore cabin.

It would cost you 4s. as a cabin passenger, or 2s. on deck to get to Newport on the *Cambria* or *St. David*. The *Cambria* on her way to Newport would take you down the Avon to Pill or Lamplighters Hall for 1s.. But if you took their rival the *Lady Rodney* it would cost you half the price.

The fares to Chepstow were as for Newport 4s. and 2s..

On the Irish routes, where the competition was fierce, the rival companies were not in the habit of disclosing their fares to the press, but used the weekly bills, which gave the times of sailing.

One bill published by the St. George Steam Packet Company of Liverpool in September, 1822, shows that you could go to Tenby as a cabin passenger for £1 5s. or to Ilfracombe for £1 1s.; if you went steerage you could go for 15s.. Dublin was £2 12s.6d. cabin, or steerage £1 11s.6d.. And Liverpool was £4 4s. or £2 5s.. Fares were also quoted for carriages, four-wheeled and two-wheeled, and dogs.

There was a certain style. The advertisement stated:

A GOOD TABLE will be served on board, with Wines of great variety, and of the first description, as well as Spirits, Ale and Porter, of the best quality, and at reasonable prices.

A comforting thought for a journey to Dublin that was expected to last for 28 hours or so.

WAR OFFICE STEAM PACKETS.
BRISTOL, DUBLIN, CORK,
and TENBY.

THE War Office Steam Packet *GEORGE IV*. JOHN BROWN, Commander, Sails from BRISTOL for CORK every SATURDAY, and leaves CORK for BRISTOL every TUESDAY.

The War Office Steam Packet *PALMERSTON*, JOHN HYDE, Commander, Sails from BRISTOL for DUBLIN every WEDNESDAY, and leaves DUBLIN for BRISTOL every SATURDAY.

These Steam Packets are built entirely of Oak, from the identical Models and Plans of the Royal Sovereign and Meteor Holyhead Post-Office Steam Packets (which from their superior construction have continued their voyages regularly through the whole winter.) They are completed with entirely new Engines of the best and most approved principles; their accommodations are arranged in Separate Cabins.

The Steam Yatch *DUKE OF LANCASTER*, JAMES COOK, Commander, Sails from BRISTOL for TENBY and DUBLIN every SATURDAY, and leaves DUBLIN for TENBY and BRISTOL every TUESDAY.

TIMES OF SAILING:
For TENBY.
Saturday, June 21, 5 o'Clock } Morning.
Ditto 28, 9 o'Clock }
Ditto July 5, 3 o'Clock Afternoon.
Ditto 12, 9 o'Clock Morning.

For DUBLIN.
Wednesday, June 18, 1 o'Clock Afternoon.
Saturday, 21, 5 o'Clock }
Wednesday, 25, 7 o'Clock } Morning.
Saturday, 28, 9 o'Clock }
Wednesday, July 2, 11 o'Clock }
Saturday, 5, 3 o'Clock Afternoon.
Wednesday, 9, 8 o'Clock } Morning.
Saturday, 12, 9 o'Clock }
Wednesday, 16, 12 o'Clock Day.

For CORK.
Saturday, June 21, 5 o'Clock } Morning.
Ditto 28, 9 o'Clock }
Ditto July 5, 3 o'Clock Afternoon.
Ditto 12, 9 o'Clock Morning.

AND REGULARLY DURING THE SEASON.

The Steam Packets *ST. DAVID* and *CAMBRIA*, to and from NEWPORT Daily (Sundays excepted.)

☞ Male and Female Attendants on board each of the above Vessels. Refreshments may be had on Board.

*** Application may be made to R. SMART, 1, Quay, Bristol, Agent to His Majesty's War-Office Packets; J. ELLIOTT, Sackville-Street, Dublin; J. N. SMART, Quay, Cork.

The Proprietors of the above Vessels beg respectfully to observe, that the PALMERSTON and DUKE OF LANCASTER are built of such a size as enables them to embark and land their Passengers at the North Wall, Dublin; whereby the Public avoid the unpleasant and dangerous landing at Dunlary in small Boats, and are saved the trouble and expence of travelling by land from thence to Dublin, the inconveniencies of which are generally complained of.

War Office Steam Packet Office, Bristol, June, 1823.

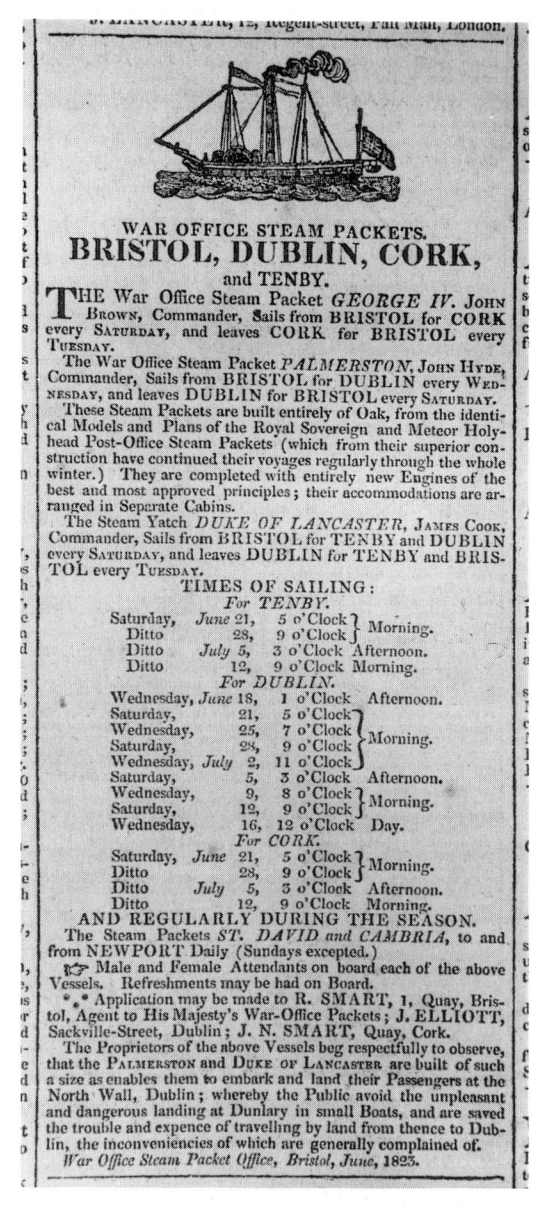

5. *S.P. Palmerston* and *George IV* advertisement: Felix Farley's Bristol Journal (by kind permission of the Bristol Reference Library). Readers enjoyed reading between the lines of the advertisements of the War Office Company and its rival the St. Patrick Company.

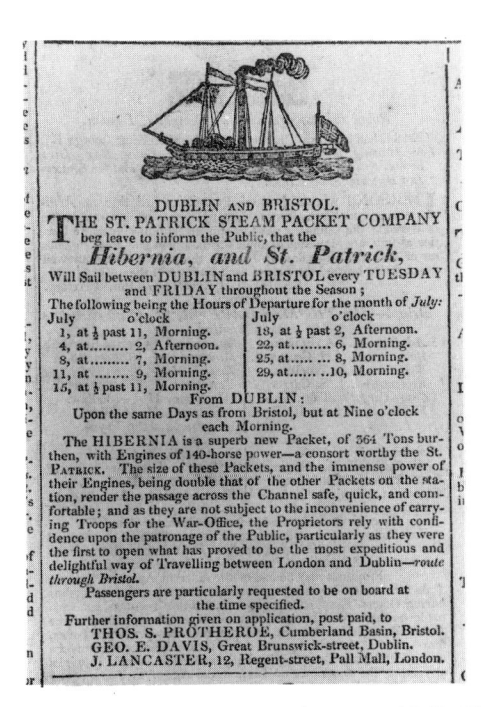

> **DUBLIN AND BRISTOL.**
>
> THE ST. PATRICK STEAM PACKET COMPANY beg leave to inform the Public, that the
>
> *Hibernia, and St. Patrick,*
>
> Will Sail between DUBLIN and BRISTOL every TUESDAY and FRIDAY throughout the Season;
>
> The following being the Hours of Departure for the month of *July:*
>
> | July | o'clock | July | o'clock |
> |---|---|---|---|
> | 1, at ½ past 11, Morning. | | 18, at ½ past 2, Afternoon. | |
> | 4, at .... 2, Afternoon. | | 22, at .... 6, Morning. | |
> | 8, at .... 7, Morning. | | 25, at .... 8, Morning. | |
> | 11, at .... 9, Morning. | | 29, at ....10, Morning. | |
> | 15, at ½ past 11, Morning. | | | |
>
> From DUBLIN:
> Upon the same Days as from Bristol, but at Nine o'clock each Morning.
>
> The HIBERNIA is a superb new Packet, of 364 Tons burthen, with Engines of 140-horse power—a consort worthy the St. PATRICK. The size of these Packets, and the immense power of their Engines, being double that of the other Packets on the station, render the passage across the Channel safe, quick, and comfortable; and as they are not subject to the inconvenience of carrying Troops for the War-Office, the Proprietors rely with confidence upon the patronage of the Public, particularly as they were the first to open what has proved to be the most expeditious and delightful way of Travelling between London and Dublin—*route through Bristol.*
>
> Passengers are particularly requested to be on board at the time specified.
>
> Further information given on application, post paid, to
> THOS. S. PROTHEROE, Cumberland Basin, Bristol.
> GEO. E. DAVIS, Great Brunswick-street, Dublin.
> J. LANCASTER, 12, Regent-street, Pall Mall, London.

6. *S.P. Hibernia* and *St. Patrick* advertisement: Felix Farley's Bristol Journal (by kind permission of the Bristol Reference Library).

Advertisements are, as Grahame Farr clearly showed, an important source of information not only about the activities of the packet companies, but also about their insecurity in the face of opposition. The companies sought to improve their image in the eyes of the public at the expense of their competitors. And their skirmishing with each other through advertisements no doubt gave great delight to the editors and amusement to the readers.

Of such skirmishes one fought between the St. Patrick Company of Liverpool and the War Office Company of Bristol during 1823 gives some idea of the tension between the companies.

The War Office Company made its thrust on behalf of the *George IV* and the *Palmerston*:

> The above excellent and beautiful Packets are built entirely of Oak, and are precisely of the same fine model, strength, and power as the Royal Sovereign Steam Packet, which conveyed

His Most Gracious Majesty KING GEORGE THE FOURTH to Dublin, on his visit to Ireland; and from not being more than two-thirds the size of the other Vessels upon the station, they consequently draw much less water, and the PALMERSTON has *therefore the decided advantage of being enabled to embark and land* her Passengers at the QUAY in the CITY of DUBLIN, and not at Dunleary, as is the case with the other Boats sailing thither. The PALMERSTON and GEORGE THE FOURTH have kept their regular and appointed days of sailing without delay, and without the slightest accident, and are navigated by Commanders of the greatest experience, who have been reared from their infancy to the Navigation between Bristol and Ireland; it is therefore respectfully hoped the Public will give preference to Vessels of their decided superiority in point of sailing and accommodation. Carriages are carefully shipped.

No horses conveyed by the above Packets, Palmerston or George the Fourth, but by sailing Vessels.

From the very extensive and liberal Patronage already conferred upon the Palmerston and George the Fourth Passengers may be assured that every exertion will be constantly made to promote their comfort, and prevent the possibility of experiencing the slightest annoyance of any kind. . . . An excellent Table kept, and Refreshments of every description.

The St. Patrick Company in its turn sought to convince all of the undoubted superiority of its ships the *St. Patrick* and the *Hibernia*:

The size and strength of these superb Packets, and the immense power of their Engines, being nearly double that of the others upon the station, render the passage across the Channel certain and regular: they are not subject to the annoyance of carrying Troops for the War Office, nor to the inconvenience of waiting for tides among the dangerous shoals of the Liffey, to take them up to Dublin, their passengers being landed at the fine harbour of Kingstown, in large commodious boats belonging to the establishment, where carriages are readily procured to convey them to Dublin, the distance being only five miles, and the road delightful. As the Packets sail punctually, Passengers are required to be on board half an hour before the time stated.

Using advertisements in this way to fight battles was expensive, and in time it was found that co-operation was more sensible and cheaper.

In these early days favourable press reports were of incalculable value. Felix Farley's Bristol Journal contained the following report in May 1823. It refers to a passage made by the *St. Patrick* when . . .

> she encountered the most heavy gale, more properly hurricane, for seven hours, that has been experienced in the Channel for 15 years; yet so little did she labour in the gale, that the passengers on board, nearly 40 in number, knew nothing of the matter, except the venerable Bishop of Meath, who being a little qualmish, came upon deck, although the sea ran so high as to wash away one of her boats out of the slings in the crane, and very much damage the other.

Much more sedate was the excursion to Chepstow reported by Felix Farley in July 1823:

> On Thursday last, 133 passengers were landed, at half past one o'clock, consisting entirely of Ladies and Gentlemen of fortune and their families, who had made Clifton their residence for the season, and as they walked up from the Packet into the town, resembled in appearance the congregation of a parish dismissed from divine worship on the hallowed sabbath, being habited in all the elegance of morning costume, and presenting a scene not less novel than interesting; all hastening to the Inns to obtain conveyances to Tintern, Windcliff, the Grotto Cottage, or some other objects of general attraction engaging every vehicle in Chepstow for that purpose. At six o'clock in the evening, the bugle sounded its loud notes of preparation, and from thence till seven all was activity to obtain the seats the company had so lately quitted. Soon as they were on board, the vessel made a short trip up the Wye to bring her bow round, and when she had brought her head to the tide, the paddles were called into action, and cheered by the music on board, bid an adieu to the Arcadian regions of Monmouthshire, and after a most delightful excursion of a few hours, arrived on the shores of the Avon, where carriages were in attendance to convey them to their respective homes.

And they took their enjoyment home with them.

J.F. Smart, a very early admirer of steam packets, but above all the Chepstow packet, expressed his ardour differently, in verse.

7. *The Duke of Beaufort passing Rownham Ferry, Hotwells*: lithograph, H. Jones, c.1825 (courtesy of Bristol Museums & Art Gallery).

Bristol & Chepstow
Steam Packet
DUKE OF BEAUFORT,

WILL START DURING THE PRESENT WEEK,
AT THE FOLLOWING HOURS;

	FROM BRISTOL.			FROM CHEPSTOW.
May		Morning.	May		Evening.
19	Monday,	11 o'Clock.	19	Monday,	½-past 7 o'Clock.
					Afternoon.
20	Tuesday,	6 —	20	Tuesday,	3 —
21	Wednesday,	7 —	21	Wednesday,	4 —
22	Thursday,	8 —	22	Thursday,	5 —
					Evening.
23	Friday,	8 —	23	Friday,	¼past 5 —
24	Saturday,	9 —	24	Saturday,	6 —
25	Sunday,	6 —	25	Sunday,	will not Sail.

Fares,
After Cabin, 4s.—Midships and Fore Cabin 3s.—Fore Deck 2s.
CHILDREN UNDER 12 YEARS OF AGE HALF PRICE.

Apply to MESSRS. JONES, Rownham Coal Wharf, Hotwells;
Mr. WM. TERRELL, on the Back, Bristol;
Or, MR. O. CHAPMAN, Chepstow.

Bristol and South Wales Steam Packet Office, May 5th, 1823. Bills may be had at Majors' Office, St. John's Steps.
☞ REFRESHMENTS MAY BE HAD ON BOARD.

8. Timetable of the Bristol & Chepstow Steam Packet *Duke of Beaufort*, 1823: (from the collections of Chepstow Museum, by courtesy of Monmouth Borough Museums Service).

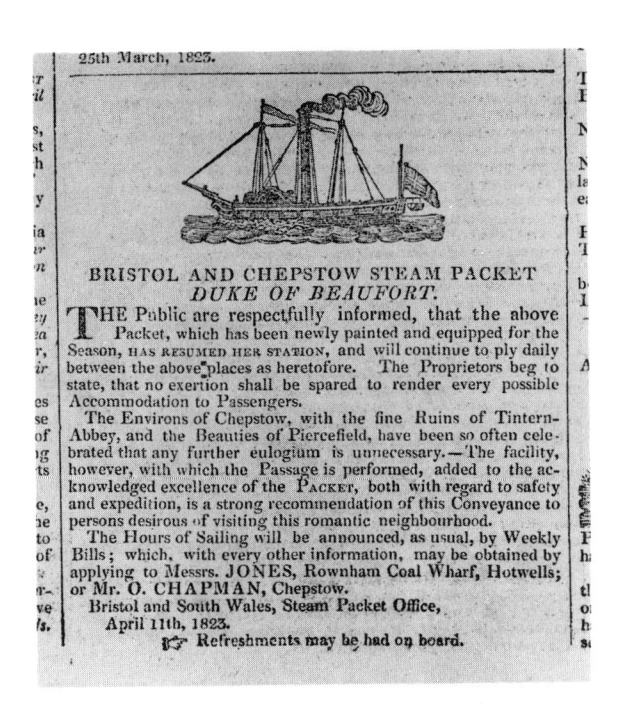

> 25th March, 1823.
>
> BRISTOL AND CHEPSTOW STEAM PACKET
> *DUKE OF BEAUFORT.*
>
> THE Public are respectfully informed, that the above Packet, which has been newly painted and equipped for the Season, HAS RESUMED HER STATION, and will continue to ply daily between the above places as heretofore. The Proprietors beg to state, that no exertion shall be spared to render every possible Accommodation to Passengers.
>
> The Environs of Chepstow, with the fine Ruins of Tintern-Abbey, and the Beauties of Piercefield, have been so often celebrated that any further eulogium is unnecessary.—The facility, however, with which the Passage is performed, added to the acknowledged excellence of the PACKET, both with regard to safety and expedition, is a strong recommendation of this Conveyance to persons desirous of visiting this romantic neighbourhood.
>
> The Hours of Sailing will be announced, as usual, by Weekly Bills; which, with every other information, may be obtained by applying to Messrs. JONES, Rownham Coal Wharf, Hotwells; or Mr. O. CHAPMAN, Chepstow.
>
> Bristol and South Wales, Steam Packet Office,
> April 11th, 1823.
>
> ☞ Refreshments may be had on board.

9. *S.P. Duke of Beaufort* advertisement: Felix Farley's Bristol Journal (by kind permission of the Bristol Reference Library).

Not at all inclined,

> '. . . To write of furnaces and flues
> Vast iron boilers, valves and screws . . .'

but rather to declare his feelings for the *Duke of Beaufort*,

> '. . . she's the magnet of our love;
> Her sheer, her beauty, and her make,
> All prove her firm and matchless shape . . .'

and surveying the passengers,

> '. . . A freight, so full of sparkling eyes . . .'

he went on to note,

> '. . . A table spread with choicest cheer;
> Tea, coffee, eggs, with capillaire,
> Ham, tongue, and rum, and bottled beer,
> For early breakfast you may take,

Or dine, or sup when passage late . . .
And now on beef and fish we dine,
And quaff the liquid of the vine:
In merry mood, and jocund ring,
Some touch the lute and others sing . . .'

Those were the palmy days. In another vein, 'We have much pleasure,' wrote the Bristol Gazette, 'in witnessing the great increase of Passengers of the first *consequence and respectability* that weekly go and arrive from DUBLIN in that beautiful Steam Packet the *Palmerston*, belonging to our spirited fellow citizens.'

To begin with the steamers worked only the better part of the year; the sailing packets took over again for the winter. It did not take more than a couple of seasons before the Newport and Chepstow packets were working winter and summer. For the Irish steam packets, however, regular winter sailings took longer to establish. The problem was ultimately one of profitability. From the passengers' point of view a winter passage was to be avoided; and they were mostly the sort of people who could choose their time. But for an unavoidable winter journey the route via Holyhead to Dublin would, perhaps, seem more attractive, since the sea passage would take about a third of the time. For the operating companies, however, it was unprofitable to keep their steamers idle in the winter. And so it was not long before the companies were forced into a radical change of policy.

At the beginning of 1823 the War Office Company had no intention of carrying cargo on its Irish steamers; it was prepared to take carriages, but the horses had to go by sailing vessel. In the search for profitability, however, style had to be sacrificed. The answer to the problem of profitability was pigs. The pig trade with Ireland was already well established. There was a strong market for them in Bristol and a plentiful supply of pigs frequently left Dublin, Cork and Waterford in sailing vessels. When a new small packet company based on Waterford used their recently acquired steamer *Nora Creina*, 202 tons, to carry a succession of cargoes of pigs to Bristol, the other companies followed. It soon became clear that no matter how few passengers travelled in the winter there would always be large numbers of pigs to be brought to Bristol winter and summer alike.

The Admiralty, only a dozen or so years after Trafalgar,

thought the chief use of steamers would be for towing men o' war out of harbour when necessary; and the Post Office with their sailing packets carrying mail, for a time thought much the same.

In Bristol with the passage down the Avon linking it with the sea, narrow and tidal, and with the wind funnelled through its gorge, the way was especially difficult for ships under sail moving between the city docks and King Road. The use of steam for towing would seem to have been obvious from the start. However things were not that simple.

The movement of ships in the port of Bristol was governed by tradition. Pilots, operating under the authority of the Society of Merchant Venturers of Bristol, moved ships not only the six miles up and down the Avon, but wherever necessary within the Bristol Channel. In fact their jurisdiction extended throughout the Channel from Gloucester to Barnstaple and similarly along the coast of South Wales.

It was hard work and the tide was a relentless taskmaster. The pilots moving ships up and down the Avon were assisted by "hobblers", men who rowed the tow-boats, and from the tow

10. *The Avon Gorge at Sunset*: Nicholas Pocock, c.1785 (The Society of Merchant Venturers, courtesy of Bristol Museums and Art Gallery) The painting illustrates the time-consuming and expensive practice of the 'hobblers'.

paths on either side of the river there were men with horses ready to take part in the operation.

These men had more than their work in common. They came from the same place, Pill, a village settled around a creek on the Somerset side of the Avon. It was a hereditary occupation they followed and, interrelated by marriage, they formed a natural brotherhood against all who threatened their livelihood.

Steam was being used for towing on the Clyde, the Mersey, the Thames and the Tyne, yet, wrote 'Cosmo', nom de plume of a stern critic of the port authorities, 'six or eight horses, and as many boats with nine men in each' might be used to tow a West Indiaman up or down the Avon when, he maintained, a steamboat of twenty horse-power would do it twice as easily and four times as cheaply.

And stories did the rounds about 'the threats of those monsters of the Avon, commonly called "Pill Sharks" '. They accorded well with the reputation of Pill men for rough language, among whom drunkenness and inefficiency were not unknown. 'Cosmo', writing in 1823, is the source of one such story.

> The captain of one of the Steam Packets which entered this harbour last summer, seeing a vessel in King road likely to lose the tide, took it in tow; for which act of kindness and consideration, he received a letter from *his own brother*, a Pill pilot, that if ever he did such an act again, his life would be in danger.

There was agitation for the introduction of steam towing from the beginning, and experiments using paddle-steamers were encouraged by Christopher Claxton and Mark Whitwell, sen.. For example, Capt. W. H. Weldy advertised the Bristol and Glamorgan Company's under used steam-packets to undertake towing from Cumberland Basin to King Road. His brave efforts, which resulted in the towing of six West Indiamen by the *Bristol* and *Glamorgan*, with help from the *George IV*, were publicly commended by Claxton, a well connected sea captain, friend and colleague of Brunel and an 'active man on all occasions – whether on land or sea'. Nevertheless, it was ten years later, in 1836, before the *Fury*, a steam-tug, started work on the Avon – and even then the men of Pill tried to scuttle her.

The notoriously difficult South Wales coast, is littered with rocks and islands, sandbanks and estuaries and tricky currents.

And the coastal inhabitants had a reputation of their own as inhospitable as their shores. They took greedily whatever the sea gave up, whole communities were involved in the plunder of shipwrecks; there was safety in numbers and authority turned a blind eye. Just occasionally the authorities would act.

Thomas Burgess, Bishop of St. David's, had extensive coastal boundaries to his diocese. From St. David's they stretched northwards to Aberystwyth and eastwards, taking in the Gower, to Swansea. Alarmed by what he heard was happening, the bishop tried in 1815 admonition through his rural deans;

> Rev. Sir,
> The disgraceful transactions, which have lately taken place on the coast of Cardiganshire and Pembrokeshire, induce me to request you to write to all the clergy of your deanery, whose parishes lie on the sea coast, and to inform them that it is my warmest wish and injunction, that they will lose no time in representing to their congregations, in terms "sharper than any two edged sword" the cruel and unchristianlike enormity of plundering wrecks; and that, for the future, they will preach to them on this subject once a quarter, or at least twice every year, and press strongly on their consciences the flagrant criminality of this inhuman practice, so disgraceful to them as Britons and Christians, to the enlightened country of which they are natives, and more especially to the neighbourhood which they inhabit, and wholly repugnant to every principle, spiritual and practical, of the benevolent religion they profess.
>
> I am, Reverend Sir,
> Your faithful and affectionate friend,
> T. St. David's

In a rare case where authority did act and the law was enforced, one is left with an uncomfortable feeling that an unfortunate fellow was left to face the full force of the law, and punished as a deterrent to the real culprits who remained free.

The case was reported in The Times:

> Thomas Moore of Moreton, labourer, was convicted at the Chester assizes of stealing ropes from the *Mary and Betsey*, stranded on the Wallasey shore in October, 1820, and sentenced to death. It is to be hoped, that all those persons who have hitherto looked upon wrecking as a lawful trade, will learn from his sentence, that by the law of the land, as well as the laws

of humanity, it is considered a most atrocious crime. By the 26th of Geo. II plundering a vessel in distress (whether wreck or no wreck) is felony without benefit of clergy.

Times were hard; and tradition has it that it was not unheard of in some parishes along the South Wales coast, that bodies washed ashore were returned to the sea again in order to avoid burial at the parish's expense.

It has to be said purely in clarification that the original War Office Steam Packet Company suffered early in its life a bewildering series of changes in title. In 1827 it became the General Steam Packet Company of Bristol; then in 1834 the Bristol Steam Packet Company; re-constituted in 1836 it took title as the Bristol General Steam Navigation Company, a title which lasted until it became finally the Bristol Steam Navigation Company about 50 years later.

The company could point to an impressive record of maintenance in the way of refits and boilers replaced. With its ships being kept busy and operating in the most testing seas, it needed to be impressive.

Among ships' engineers employed by the company from the early days were a number of Scotsmen. In addition there were local men originally firemen or stokers who had been promoted. Experience of steam engines was to be gained locally in factories and mills, distilleries and collieries in and around Bristol. And notably in Cheese Lane, St. Philip's there was Winwood's which had been in the business of making steam engines for 40 years or more before steamers came to Bristol.

The absence of serious boiler explosions on Bristol steamers at this period would seem to indicate good engine-room practice. There were a number of horrific explosions on board steamers elsewhere that were attributable directly to lax discipline and ignorance. In such cases putting extra weights on to the safety valves and forgetting 'to let off steam' when stationary were likely malpractices. Where racing was involved as well such malpractices were even more likely to end in disaster.

It seems the custom was formed early for captains to keep clear of the engine-room, and leave that department entirely to the engineers. George Bailey of the *Killarney* is a good example of that.

The first masters of War Office steam packets had changed

over from sailing packets. Men like James Cooke, formerly master of the *Marquis of Wellington*, became master of the *Duke of Lancaster*; John Brown moved from the *Marquis of Anglesea* to take over the *George IV*; and John Hyde of the *Shamrock* became first master of the *Palmerston*. They were the 'Commanders of the greatest experience. . . .' Appointed by the company their judgment was trusted, and when in trouble they were supported.

The excitement created by steamers on the Thames was considerable; from the watermen and lightermen whose lives and livelihood were put at risk by them, to the passengers who thrilled at being on board a racing steamer.

Passengers using Bristol in 1823 were no different. In the early days when competition was fierce racing was an issue. The proprietors of the *Lady Rodney* magisterially stated their position:

> Many persons having expressed their fears that accidents might arise if *racing* were to take place between the boats on this station, the proprietors wish to assure their Friends and the Public, that nothing of the kind shall be permitted with their Packet.

Within a month of this announcement an incident had taken place that revealed the dangers. It was not racing but a collision between the *Hibernia*, 3 miles off Milford on her way to Dublin, and her sister-ship the *St. Patrick* bound for Bristol. It is alleged that both were going at 10 m.p.h..

Apparently the *Hibernia* was struck by the *St. Patrick*'s bow on her starboard quarter and extensively damaged.

With wonderful understatement, a passenger on the *Hibernia* noted the *St. Patrick* bore down, 'wishing I suppose to speak (with) us . . . one would have thought the sea was wide enough for both vessels.'

But a passenger was killed. Mr. Thomas Swap, travelling for Messrs. Deacon, Sons & Ellis of Cateaton St., London, was sitting on deck when he was fatally struck.

There were the usual commercial niggles and sharp practice, like this one:

> In consequence of placards having been circulated stating that "the Chepstow Steam Packet sails daily from *Bathurst Basin*," the Proprietors of the DUKE OF BEAUFORT, with a view to

prevent the Public being misled, beg to state that *their Packet* sails regularly *from* and *to* the HOTWELLS as heretofore; that being in every respect the most convenient place, as on an average one hour and a half is gained on the passage, independent of its sometimes being found impracticable to reach Chepstow from Bathurst Basin, or to return thither on one tide; circumstances which give to the HOTWELLS as the place of starting, a decided advantage, the Duke of Beaufort having made her passages on all occasions with regularity, and without subjecting her passengers to disappointment or delay.

Things were happening in 1823, but not fast enough for 'Cosmo' who in a series of well argued letters, spiced with humour, sharply attacked the Mayor and Corporation, the Docks Company and the Society of Merchant Venturers for their management of the port.

On the quayside only those who were up and about their business at Cumberland Basin early in the morning would have witnessed the scene between the new dockmaster and the agent for the Bristol and Glamorgan Steam Packet Company. Those who did not hear the story, had a chance later of reading about it, for it emerged from a case in the Quarter Sessions, William Upton Eddis v Martin Hilhouse.

It transpired that Eddis, himself a former ship's master, had arrived at 5.20 a.m. on the quayside to discover the Swansea packet, *Glamorgan*, had just cast off, under the orders of Hilhouse, the dockmaster, and was under way towards the river Avon through the dock gates. Eddis, as agent, had come to oversee the arrangements on her. He knew the captain was not on board, neither were the passengers; the *Glamorgan* had not taken on coal and was not due to sail for another hour.

Eddis shouted to the mate to throw him a rope. The dockmaster intervened angrily, "Do you tell 'em to hold on, when I have thrown off!" he shouted at Eddis. Then proceeding to use 'his fistic powers' to enforce his orders, he clouted Eddis twice, following it by 'the expression of an intended application to that part of [Eddis'] person which is generally denominated the *seat of honour*.'

For the dock master, connected as he was 'by family ties to the magistracy of the city', it was humiliating. He was fined £10. The incident was trivial in itself. But it showed that there was a lot to be learnt.

And now to serious matters.

All the stories which follow are about paddle-steamers which belonged to the Bristol General Steam Navigation Company or its predecessors. These 'early Bristol paddle-steamers' were all wooden-hulled and operating in the hey-day of packet steamer activity – a time before the iron-framed pier gave holiday crowds greater access to the paddle-steamer and pleasure cruises in the Bristol Channel.

1. The *Frolic*

[Built at Greenock, 1827.
108 tons; length 112′; breadth 18′6″; depth 10′4″; 1 deck and a quarter-deck; 2 masts; schooner rig; square stern; mock galleries; man figurehead.]
    Farr: West Country Passenger Steamers, pp.77 & 302

In 1830 the directors of the General Steam Navigation Company of Bristol, as the company was then called, were in a strong position. They had overcome their rivals, the Bristol & Glamorgan Steam Packet Company, on the Bristol – Swansea route, after a fierce struggle and were keen to expand. The idea was to develop a new steam packet service from Bristol to the far west of Wales.

At this time the Post Office ran a daily steam packet service carrying the mail from Milford to Waterford. Despite that official recognition, it has to be said that the facilities at Milford were woefully inadequate. There was no pier at Milford. The packets lay ½ to ¾ mile off shore in a safe anchorage. The mail had to be transferred by boat. It was difficult for the packets to take on board stores, coal, carriages and horses, and passengers, especially in bad weather. The great attraction that Milford had for the Post Office was its deep water, which meant that the packets could sail with the mail without having to delay for the tide, a facility that Bristol could not offer. But because of the lack of a pier at Milford, it had been reluctantly decided, after a thorough investigation led by Thomas Telford, to build a quay at Hobbs Point on the Pembroke Dock side of the Haven and to move the Post Office packet station there from Milford. The work was in progress.

Nevertheless, the plan to make a steam packet link between Bristol and Milford Haven was sound. Bristol was the commercial centre for shopkeepers and tradespeople in the west of Wales. For such people to go to see for themselves what was available in Bristol and bring back bulky purchases by steamer was a new

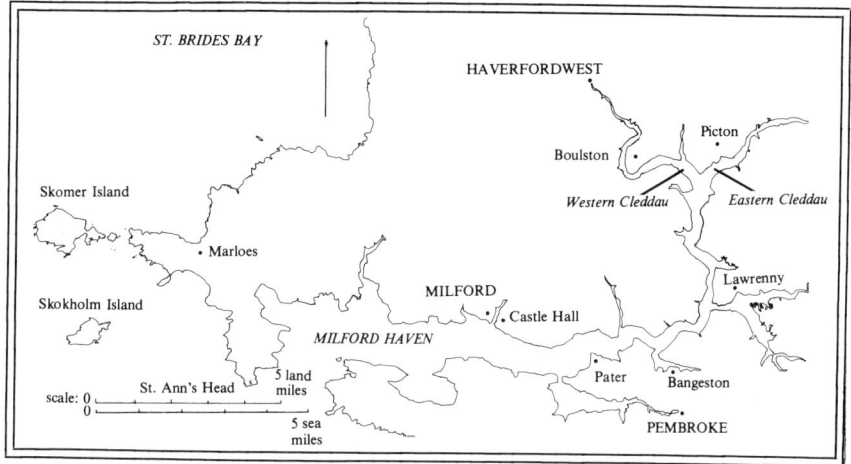

Map 2: Milford Haven: showing also the islands of Skomer and Skokholm.

possibility. As a means of travel it would have a special attraction for those who found coach travel unbearable, particularly as they would also avoid the dreaded crossing of the Severn.

To this end the company bought the *Frolic*, a wooden hulled paddle-steamer with 80 h.p. engines. Not a new ship, she had served an apprenticeship of three years on the route between Glasgow and Belfast.

The new owners intended the *Frolic* to sail Bristol to Tenby, calling alternately at Carmarthen one week and Haverfordwest the next, making stops at Milford and on the Pembroke side of the Haven on its way there. The company was already well acquainted with Tenby, it being a stopping place for Irish packets on occasion and linked some summers with Ilfracombe.

The *Frolic* had begun establishing her run in November 1830, not the best time of year to start a new service. It appears that Carmarthen was soon dropped from her schedule, no doubt for commercial reasons.

However, be that as it may, Felix Farley's Bristol Journal for 12 March, 1831, carried the following advertisement:

'For Haverfordwest, calling at Tenby, – The *Frolic*'

For Haverfordwest Fridays:	From Haverfordwest Tuesdays:
March 18, 8 morning.	March 15, 7 morning.
March 25, 4 afternoon	March 22, 12 noon

35

'Passengers and goods ... a female steward ... horses and carriages shipped with care.'

It is with the sailing from Haverfordwest advertised for Tuesday, March 15 at 7 in the morning that we are concerned here.

The *Frolic* had been sailing throughout the winter, and the winter was now nearly over.

Her master, Edward Jenkins, once a serving Lieutenant of the Royal Navy, lived in Back Street, Haverfordwest, apparently in a corner cottage almost opposite the Mariner's Hotel. He had been long experienced in the coasting trade with Bristol.

On board there was with him a crew of thirteen and an experienced Channel pilot. It is said that two of the crew had also been Channel pilots at one time.

It is not by any means certain that the *Frolic* was in the habit of sailing up the river Cleddau to Haverfordwest. Oral tradition suggests that she was not; although it is claimed that ships up to 200 tons could reach Haverfordwest on spring tides. The narrowness and lack of depth in the river would have made manoeuvring exceptionally difficult for a paddle-steamer. There is documentary evidence that later successors, the *Phoenix* and the *Star*, lay where the Cleddau opens out into the Haven and were served by a lighter which came down the river from the quay at Haverfordwest.

However, be that as it may, on the day in question the *Frolic* had on board passengers from Haverfordwest, Pembroke, Milford and Tenby. There would seem to have been little hurry in the business of taking on passengers and goods. There is nothing to suppose that there was anything unusual in this part of the proceedings on that day.

However, from the time the *Frolic* left Tenby nothing more was heard of her until the news reached Bristol on Thursday, 17 March; that is two days after the first move was made away from the quay at Haverfordwest.

The *Bristol*, the Swansea steam packet, on her way back to Bristol, when passing Nash Sands off the inhospitable Glamorgan coast found her way impeded by floating wreckage. Her captain reported seeing a paddle-box on the shore, and the boiler and part of an engine on the sand banks. With the *Frolic* overdue there could be little doubt they belonged to her.

Further confirmation came from the *City of Bristol*, on her way home from Cork. She reported seeing a paddle-box on the sands, and the sea strewn with floating wreckage, bedding and stores.

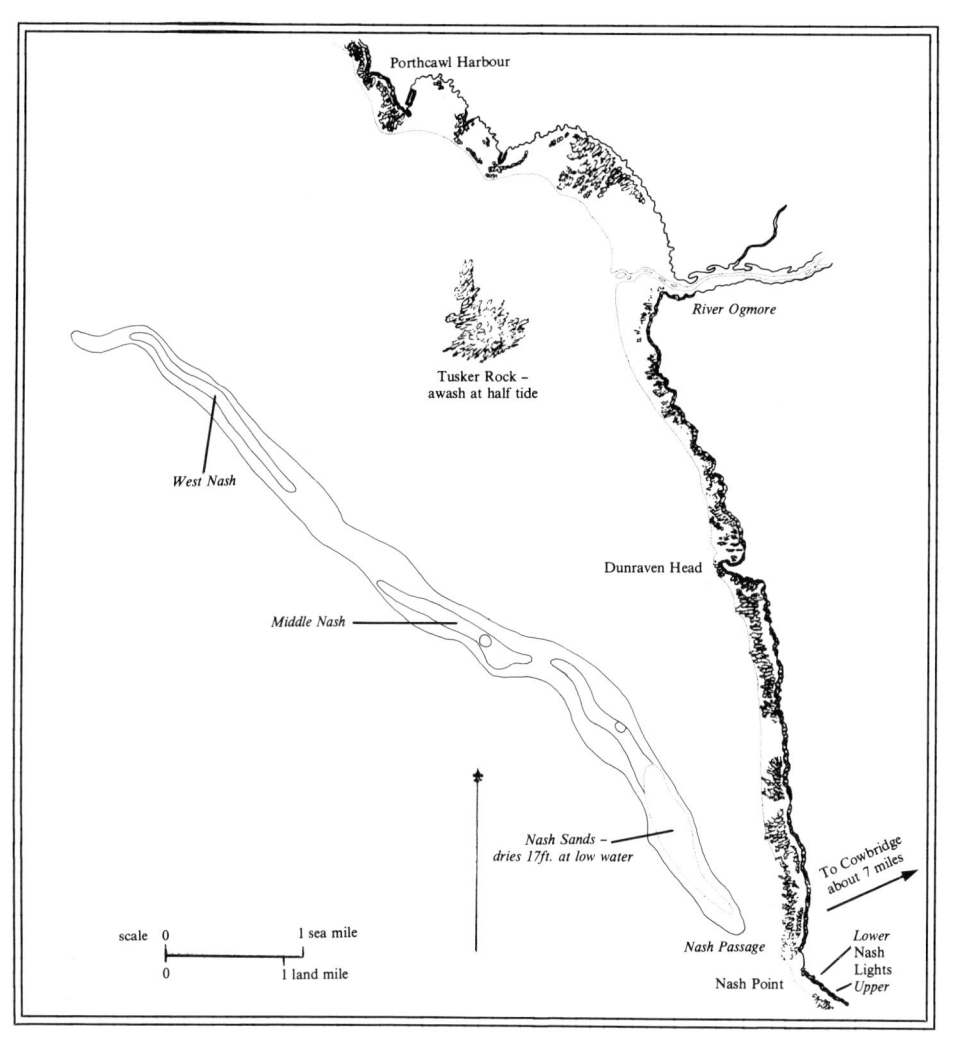

Map 3: Nash Sands, based on Denham's chart: here the *Frolic* was lost in 1831. Note Nash Lights which began operating the following year.

The guard of the Milford mail said he had heard on the way at Cowbridge of wreckage being washed up.

In Bristol the news caused a sensation. Each arrival of the Welsh mail was awaited with anxiety for further news of the disaster. By now it was clear there were no survivors.

It was assumed, in the absence of any witnesses, that the *Frolic* and all those on board had perished during the dark hours of the

Wednesday night or the Thursday morning, 16/17 March. A 'dark, dirty and tempestuous' night it was, blowing a gale and with hazy visibility.

In its own time the sea gave up its dead, and with them one or two clues.

The body of the captain was washed up, and was found lashed to the rigging. His watch, it was discovered, had stopped a few minutes short of 4 o'clock. Also lashed to the rigging was a young boy; and a young woman was discovered with a child still wrapped secure in her arms.

Clearly it was no sudden disaster.

Various opinions were expressed. It was suggested that the *Frolic*, in trouble, stood off Nash Sands waiting for daybreak when overtaken by events. One nautical view was that the *Frolic* would have gone over the moment she struck.

Local opinion, however, favoured the view that she was in desperate trouble before she struck. High seas, strong winds and the darkness gave added terror to the sands. It was noted that the anchor cable had snapped leaving some 12 fathoms still suspended from the wreck; and, further, that the anchor itself was found quite separately with 40 fathoms of chain attached to it. From this it was deduced that the anchor might well have been used in unsuitable conditions. This would suggest that the captain was forced to resort to frantic measures.

Maybe the engines suffered mechanical failure; or the *Frolic* shipped water and as a consequence the fires were put out. With his ship powerless, perhaps the captain felt constrained to drop his anchor. And could it be that the anchor became fouled and tore out the bows? Who knows?

'The vicinity of Cowbridge evinces a truly melancholy appearance,' it was reported. 'Groups of persons are continually wandering about the beach in search of the bodies of their relatives and friends.'

A Miss Henderson was found by her friends, with her two trunks nearby. She was fully clothed; but the fact that her boots were unlaced drew the suggestion that she was in bed when the crisis occurred.

But for those without personal considerations to attend to the immediate question was, how many were there on board?

At once it emerged that there was no passenger list of any kind.

Felix Farley, published two days after the news reached Bristol, stated the ship's company to be fifteen. The paper went on, 'rumour states there were forty passengers on board. This, however, we hope and trust is an exaggeration, as the vessel rarely had so many passengers.'

A week later, The Cambrian, a newspaper published at Swansea, reported, 'It is impossible to state accurately how many were on board, and there are very contradictory reports in circulation; but from the best information that we can collect, the number of passengers is estimated to be about forty and the crew about fifteen.'

Nobody really knew.

However, The Bristol Gazette and Public Advertiser produced as evidence a letter 'from a respectable individual residing in Haverfordwest'. Written four days after the wreck, he said that it was generally believed there that between seventy and eighty people had perished.

Clearly this was a sensitive matter in Bristol. The paper took pains to discount this estimate,.'... we are glad to say that the Steam Packet Company, who ought to possess the best information, think that number to be much overrated.'

By searching through a variety of contemporary newspapers it has been possible to establish a list of passengers. It was the 'respectable individual from Haverfordwest' who was about right.

From Haverfordwest it is reckoned twelve people embarked. Of these three were seamen from Fishguard, Davis, Dunn (or Drum) and Moore; two more were servants from Picton Castle, the seat of Sir Richard Philipps, M.P., one of them being Hester Turner, a maid of twenty-five; then there was Mr. James Lloyd, butler to R.J. Acland, Esq., of Boulston, and a Mr. John Barthum of London, formerly of Lawrenny. From Haverfordwest itself, Mr. James Griffiths, like his father a currier and leatherseller of Prendergast; Mr. George Evans, (?tin-plate worker), and Ann Griffiths of Portfield. From Clarbeston there was Mr. W. Griffiths of Pentypark Mill.

Off H.M. Dockyard at Pembroke Dock a further six passengers embarked. Three were Bennett, Richards and George, runaway apprentices of J. Mathias, (?shoemaker); Miss Henderson, aged 19, and her brother Thomas, aged 20, whose father, W. Henderson, Esq., of Bangeston, was contractor for the dockyard works then going on at Hobbs Point; and a Mr. George of Pater (pronounced 'Patter', being the local abbreviation for Peterchurch, the old name for what is now called Pembroke Dock).

Twenty-two passengers boarded the *Frolic* off Milford. Mrs. Hardway (or Holloway), a housemaid, and Mr. Jenkins, a butler, both from London, were leaving their places with Capt. Robert Fulke Murray Grenville at Castle Hall. Miss Mary Legge, 'a fine young woman of 18 years of age', and the niece of Capt. Pedbury, R.N., a merchant of Milford, was being chaperoned by Mrs. Reynish (?Greenish), wife of a butcher in the town. In addition there was a group of eighteen sailors on their way to join the South Sea Whalers.

At Tenby a maximum of twenty-three persons joined the ship: among them General McLeod, said to be of the 1st. Royal Regiment of Foot, and with him four servants; Mrs. Boyd, wife of a Colonel, accompanied by her niece, Miss Richardson, and three servants; a Colonel Gordon, late of the Queen's Bays, with one or two servants; two children and seven or eight others all unknown.

Taken together these figures produce a maximum of sixty-three passengers. With a crew of fifteen, it would seem reasonably certain that there were not more than seventy-eight people on board.

Of the crew, most of them remain unknown. The captain, Edward Jenkins, left a widow 'large in the family way', with eight children, another child of theirs was buried two days after the disaster.

The mate, who came from Pill, near Bristol, left a widow and five children.

The steward, Thomas Richard, left four children with his widow expecting their fifth. A subscription was raised on his behalf in Haverfordwest, Sir Richard Philipps, the town's M.P., giving £20.

Mrs. Boyd, the stewardess, was the wife of Mr. Boyd, hairdresser, of Narrow-wine Street in Bristol. It was said that she had been in delicate health and that her situation had been procured for her in the hope of her recovery.

Of the rest, tradition has it that one member of the crew was named Blynman. Some bodies found certain burial; Mary and Thomas Henderson at Cowbridge, Hester Turner at St. Athan, and James Lloyd was reported to have been buried at St. Brides in Glamorgan. Others unknown were buried in parishes along the coast; one bearing the initials 'J. G.'; and another, whose cork shoe was held as the only means of identification by the sexton at Cadoxton, was buried there.

*

There were some positive reactions to this terrible tragedy.

Capt. Walter Forman, R.N., of Pilton, near Shepton Mallet, put forward the idea of constructing a vessel with two keels, one under each bilge, so that in the event of the vessel taking ground she would not fall over broadside.

'Agenor' from Loughor, writing in The Cambrian, made an interesting suggestion. There were, he stated, only two safe harbours between Bristol and Milford; that is King Road and Milford Haven. He favoured a shelter midway between them on the north side of Worm's Head. It was, he went on, an ideal situation free from currents, sheltered from all winds, a depth of 20 to 30 feet at low water and a bottom of soft blue clay. With a pier or breakwater constructed there it would make a fine harbour.

In the event, however, it was the problem created by Nash Sands which received immediate and practical response. The sands off Nash Point are extensive. Today they stretch for about seven and a half miles and are in three parts. They consist of sand and gravel.

Apparently it was the custom in fair weather for paddle-

11. *Nash Sands Lighthouses*: engraving after W.H. Bartlett, 1841. The lighthouses were operating the year after the *Frolic* was lost on the Sands.

staeamers to avoid the obstruction of the sands by using Nash Passage. This passage about a cable broad, with a depth of more than three fathoms in the fairway, lies between the rocky ledge on which Nash Point rests and the sands.

A fair distance was saved by using the passage. And with their low engine efficiency and consequent high fuel costs, for paddle-steamers this was an important consideration.

As a result of public alarm arising from the disaster, Trinity House made it known that it was intending to build a lighthouse on Nash Point forthwith.

Actually Trinity House had been in touch with the Society of Merchant Venturers of Bristol on the matter only the previous year. Whether the decision had been made before the *Frolic* was wrecked is not clear.

Nevertheless the work was completed the following year to the designs of James Walker, chief engineer to Trinity House. His plans provided for the erection of two towers at Nash Point. Set one thousand feet apart, the eastern tower light had a range of nineteen miles and the western light a range of eighteen miles.

For the General Steam Navigation Company of Bristol the loss of the *Frolic* was a shattering blow.

But the company soon declared its resolve to resume its packet service to Tenby.

Barely a month after, The Cambrian carried the following advertisement:

'Bristol to Tenby in TEN HOURS with Passengers, Goods, Live Stock &tc. . . . The commodious and elegantly fitted up Steam Packet The *George IV* of 260 tons, 100 h.p. . . .

Tenby to Bristol	Bristol to Tenby
Tuesdays weekly	Saturdays weekly
All Day-light Passages and gentlemen	Separate cabins for ladies

Fares

Best cabins	£1	1s.	6d.	Fat cattle	15s.	0d.
Steerage		14s.	6d.	Store	10s.	0d.
Children under 12 half price				2-yr. old	7s.	6d.
4-Wheel carriage	£2	0s.	0d.	Yearlings	5s.	0d.
2-Wheel carriage	£1	5s.	6d.	Pigs	2s.	0d.
Horses	£1	5s.	0d.	Sheep	1s.	0d.
Dogs		3s.	0d.			

'Freight same as sailing vessels.'

Clearly the company had faith in the enterprise despite the setback.

In Pembrokeshire there was enterprise too. A largely local syndicate had been formed to rival the General Steam Navigation Company of Bristol's steam packet to West Wales. The syndicate took delivery of the *County of Pembroke*, which was Bristol built at the Wapping yard of Messrs Patterson and Mercer, later famed as builders of the *Great Western*. She was registered at Milford in August, 1831, at 110 tons with a length of 109 feet. The aim was to provide a service from Haverfordwest, Pembroke and Milford, to Bristol, leaving Tenby to the *George IV*.

Chief among the owners were Joseph Toombs, grocer, and Thomas Richards, senior, master mariner, whose son and namesake was the first master, both of Haverfordwest: and Thomas Cory, merchant, of Bristol. Other owners were as follows:

From Haverfordwest
William Owen, cabinet maker
Thomas Mathias, esquire
Daniel Lewis, draper
James Davies, draper
Thomas Beynon, maltster

Thomas Owen, merchant
George Phillips, draper
William Gibbs, watchmaker
William Crunn, gentleman
Ann Morris, spinster

John & David Jardine, merchants

From Pembroke
Richard Ormond, draper

From Pembroke Dock
Thomas West, gentleman

From Milford
Gayer Starbuck, merchant
Wm. Roberts, shipbuilder
George Paynter, merchant

From Bristol
Robert Firke, grocer
John Wells, grocer
Frederick Beeson, wharfinger
Richard Ferris, druggist
John David Jones, gentleman
William Chubb, sailmaker
James Williams, gentleman

Thus life went on and renewed activity pushed the *Frolic* disaster into the background. The year 1831 is remembered for the intense excitement in the country over the business of Parliamentary reform, and marked in Bristol particularly by the very serious riots there.

By a stroke of fortune a contemporary ballad telling the story of the *Frolic*'s last voyage has survived through oral tradition. It provides a fitting ending to the story.

Come you that got a feeling heart,
Now listen unto me,
I will tell you of a dreadful thing
That happened on the sea.

It is of the *Frolic* steam packet,
A vessel fine and gay,
From Haverfordwest to Bristol,
Believe me what I say.

She left the Port of Milford
On March the 14th day,
From Milford Town to Bristol bound,
And on Wednesday bore away.

Up around St. Govan's Head she went,
While the wind blew brisk and fair,
And Tenby Town was soon in view;
A flag was hoisted there.

Many rich gentlemen were on board
And ladies fair also,
Feared not old Neptune or his flood,
But all resolved to go.

She stopped a while at Tenby,
Then up the Channel bore.
The *Frolic* struck on Nash's sands
And never was seen any more.

Such dreadful situation which
No one could express,
And no one to relieve them
In their deep distress.

For round them was wide ocean,
And above them the blue sky;
No assistance could be given them
In their dire extremity.

And now my song is ended
And no more can I tell
Of the seventy-one poor souls who were lost
And bid this world farewell!

2. The *Albion*

[Built at Bristol, 1831.
No. 35, 1 Oct. 1831.
270* tons; length 150′ 9″; breadth (above) 25′ 2″; height 6′ 6″; 2 decks; 2 masts; schooner rig; square stern; quarter galleries; woman head; steam vessel.]
    Farr: Records of Bristol Ships; B.R.S. vol. XV.

'On Tuesday last,' declared Felix Farley's Bristol Journal in its issue of Saturday, 9th July, 1831, 'at one o'clock, was launched from the Steam Packet Company's Dock, the *Albion* steamer of 200 horse power. She went off the stocks in magnificent style, amidst the firing of cannon, and the exultations of the surrounding spectators; the band of the 3rd Regiment of light dragoons, now stationed in this city, playing several delightful airs, on the deck of a sister steamer which was moored close to her, contributing greatly to enlivening the occasion.'

This was a moment of glory before she started as a working ship. Over the past four years or so it had become the established practice for Irish steam packets to carry pigs. It was not a point that was touched on at all in the advertisements naturally. But the companies in search of profitability had come to see that steamers were particularly suitable for the movement of livestock in bulk, above all pigs.

Competition had kept passenger fares low. Passengers and deadweight cargoes simply did not generate enough income to keep the Irish packet services profitable. The fact that the shipping of pigs by steamer and the establishment of winter sailing by them came at roughly the same time was no coincidence.

Irish dealers found that steamers could take twice the number

---

*This tonnage and other tonnages where necessary have been rounded off.

12. Model of Paddle-Steamer: photograph (reproduced by permission of the Trustees of the Science Museuem). The model is a contemporary one, it seems, of a wooden-hulled paddle-steamer; it was obtained from Bristol. Of such Bristol steamers, the registration details suggest the most likely subject for the model would be either the *Albion* or the *Killarney*. That was the opinion of Grahame Farr.

carried by the sailing ships, and deliver them in hours rather than days or possibly even weeks. The arrangements, incidentally better for the pigs, were also much more satisfactory for Bristol dealers, who received large quantities of pigs delivered regularly for them to supply cheaper meat to the growing markets in Bristol. And more Bristol butchers called themselves "pork butcher".

The *Albion* soon made her mark with some fast passages. The press took notice of a particular succession of them, and Farr quotes one report with delight, "There is no equal to this and the packet must have *went* at the rate of eleven miles per hour."

Like all the steamers of the Bristol General Steam Navigation Company, the *Albion* was well maintained. Fitted with two-cylinder engines, she had undergone, in 1835, a thorough refit which had included two new boilers. In September, 1836, she had equalled the record for Dublin to Bristol in $21\frac{1}{2}$ hours.

However, we are here concerned with her in the month of April, 1837. Among the usual packet companies' advertisements in the press for that month, the *Albion* was advertised to sail for Dublin on Saturdays from the Cumberland Basin in Bristol. She was, it said, 'fitted up for the conveyance of passengers and goods . . . Horses and carriages to be shipped Two Hours before Sailing.'

Her master was George Bailey and he had a crew of 20. George Bailey, who lived at 7, Caroline Place, Hotwells, was well known for his bravery. As mate of the *George IV* he had led the daring rescue of the *Earl of Liverpool*, one of Bristol's great ships, crippled off Minehead in a gale, while returning to Bristol from New York in November, 1824. Dragging her anchor, with her mainmast cut down to stop her drift towards the Culver Sand in mid-Channel, and with the rest of her rigging going, the *Earl of Liverpool* was at the mercy of wind and sea. Encouraged by the judgment of Capt. Brown, George Bailey with men from the *George IV*, which had come up, at great risk took a ship's boat and managed to establish a line and salvage her. Within a year George Bailey had been promoted to become master of the *Palmerston*.

Like all the Irish packets the *Albion* was a busy ship. For example, on 13 April, she was back in Bristol from Dublin with passengers and goods. Her cargo: 10 bales, 2 boxes and 1 truss merchandise: 11 boxes and 5 bales linen; 1 (?box) tabbinetts; 15 hogsheads Guiness & Co.'s Extra Stout; 7 sacks malt; 1 puncheon whiskey; 4 jars sweet spirits of nitre; 6 bottles sulphuric ether; 50 tierces beef; 1 truss woollens; 419 pigs.

Two days later the *Albion* was sailing again for Dublin. This time carrying apart from passengers of course: 1 board mahogany; 236 sacks flax seed; 3 sacks clover seed; 332 bars and 30 bundles iron; 5 tierces bastard sugar; 11 mats; 2 cases floor cloth; 1 box lead; 2 hogsheads and 2 tierces refined sugar; 17 baskets cheese; 1 pack veneers; 3 boxes confectionery; 2 hampers glass; 8 baskets plants; 5 hampers cheese; 10 trusses woollens; 1 copper rod.

Her next journey was her last. She had taken on board at Dublin passengers, among them a few clergymen and army officers, and their ladies and Mr. Sergeant Jackson, M.P. for Bandon. Chief among the cargo were pigs, about 400 of them, and a quantity of spirits and porter.

It was Tuesday, 18 April, 1837, and things were going smoothly enough as the *Albion* reached the Pembrokeshire coast.

But let a passenger tell the story:

'We proceeded down the Channel at the rate of 11 miles an hour, and had every prospect of anchoring in Bristol at 5 o'clock the next morning; at 3 o'clock p.m., we came in sight of the coast of Wales, and the weather being remarkably fine,

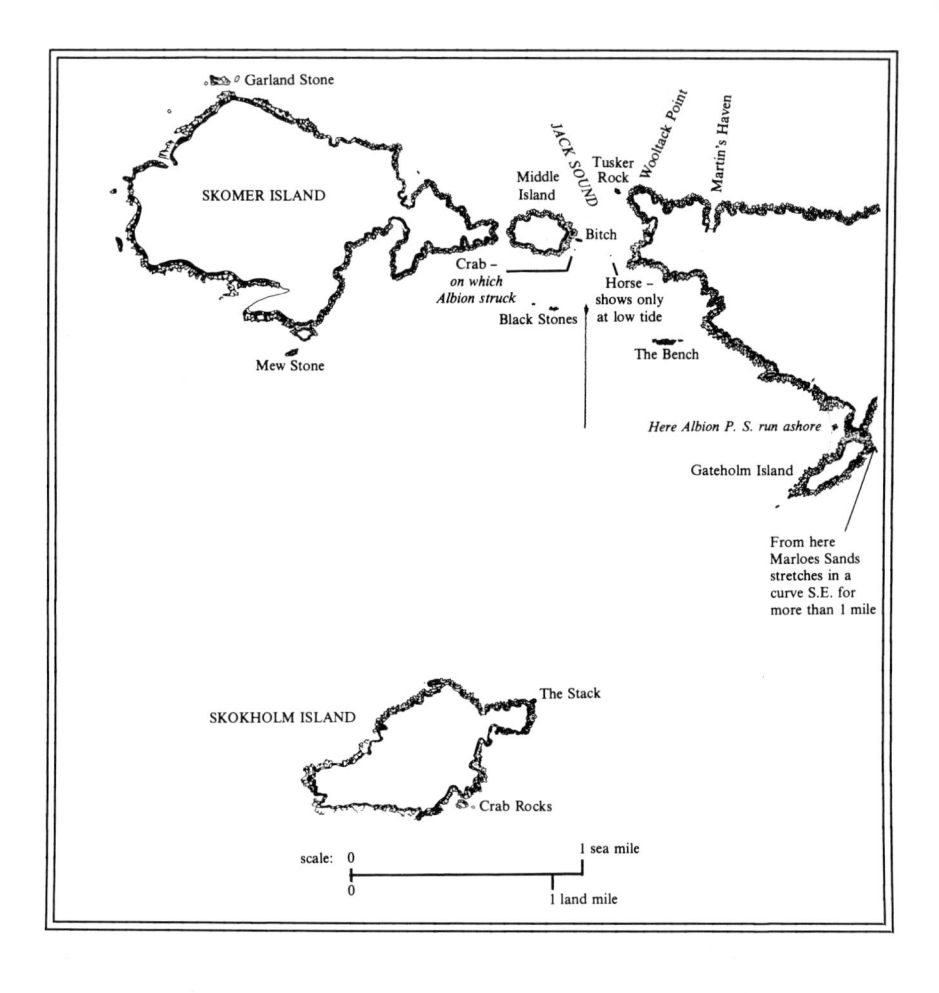

Map 4: Jack Sound: based largely on the Admiralty survey of 1830 by Denham, 1837 edition. Denham has marked where the Albion struck and where she was run aground.

Captain Bailey, in order to save time, determined to run inside the islands; we passed several in fine style, delighted with the novel scenery, until we came to a very narrow channel called Jack's Sound.

'M. and myself were seated at the stern, watching the progress of the vessel, when she struck on some sunken rocks with a dreadful crash, and immediately heeled over almost on her beam ends; the people all rushed to the other side, and the paddles continuing to work, she got off the rock, righted, and plunged into deep water. There was now a general cry that the vessel was sinking; we still, however, made way, got out of the strait and entered a bay almost one-fourth of a mile long, surrounded on all sides by inaccessible rocks except one small place which appeared all but inaccessible; the captain gave orders to run her in here. Just as she reached it (five minutes after she struck), the water reached the fires and put them out.'

The bay was part of Marloes Sands to the west of St. Ann's Head and the entrance to Milford Haven.

'On the vessel getting into shallow water, she gave one lurch then righted, and remained firm. Previous to this there had been a great rush to the boats, which would have been both immediately swamped, had it not been for the cool and determined conduct of the crew and captain – their conduct, as well as that of the helmsman, deserves the greatest praise. The boat was soon hoisted out, and the females lowered into it; the swell was dreadful, and the danger (as of course you know) very great; the boat was nearly swamped three times in landing them.

'Soon after a sloop came into sight, hove-to as near as she could, and brought most of those remaining round to Milford. I, of course, did not go on board, but asked the captain to put me on shore, which he instantly ordered a boat to do. I found M. at a farmhouse; we had to climb over rocks more than 100 feet high.'

A more emotional account of events was given by a passenger named Cunningham which was also quoted in the press.

'. . . the water rushing in upon the boiler fires, put a stop to the working of the engines, and it was with great difficulty she was run upon a rock a short distance from the place of accident. The interval of time which took place in this attempt was most awful, and the passengers manifested the utmost anxiety – amidst the escape of the steam, volumes of suffocating smoke, issuing from the lower part of the vessel as the water came in contact with the fires, darkened and obscured surrounding objects; destruction appeared inevitable – every moment was an age of intense suffering – at one period all was thought to be lost!

'Several clergymen were on board, who, falling on their knees, were joined by the passengers generally in ardent supplication to their Heavenly Father for mercy in their perilous strait – happily their prayer was heard – not one perished.

'There were 50 passengers on board; 25 belonging to the cabin, amongst whom were Col. Kirby and four other officers, the Rev. W. Le Poer French (?Trench), the Rev. – Middlecot, the Rev. – Pounder, with several ladies and children; all of whom after considerable exertion were safely taken on shore, which was bounded by a range of high and precipitous rocks, over which they were obliged to scramble and climb; fortunately the whole party received the most humane and hospitable treatment from a Welch farmer in the neighbourhood.

'Nearly all the luggage and the moveables of the steamer were saved, together with about 180 pigs and 5 horses. It was considered by the passengers that no blame attached to Capt. Bailey, who was endeavouring to make as quick a passage as possible, and whose conduct in the greatest emergency, was one means of saving their life and property.'

Other reports say 250 pigs were saved and, apart from all the ship's plate, a good quantity of the luggage and the bedding was saved.

Certainly the 'proper authorities' were soon on the scene to secure the wreck of the *Albion* and the remains of her cargo. For a short while it was thought that the hull might be floated off. From Bristol came Mr. Gilmore, one of the owners; and it was he, no doubt, who gave the authority which enabled much of the cargo to be sold on the spot.

Then the sea got to work on the *Albion*. Within days, it was reported that her deck was blown up, her bows staved and her deckhouses washed up on shore. The *Albion*, which had reputedly cost £20,000, had gone to pieces leaving the company, which insured its own ships, with a loss of £15,000 or so, it was said.

However, the story does not end quite there.

About three weeks after the event, Felix Farley's Bristol Journal, under the heading 'Ship News', contained the following paragraph without further comment:

'The unfortunate loss of the *Albion* steam vessel was occasioned by a boat with four men in it, crossing immediately before the vessel's bows, by which Capt. Bailey was reduced to the necessity of either running her down, or altering his course; he adopted the latter alternative and starboarded the helm, but by this circumstance the *Albion* was brought so close in that the tide took her starboard bow, and she refused to answer the helm, and immediately struck.'

This is curious. The incident was not mentioned in either of the passengers' accounts as printed in the newspapers immediately after. Jack Sound was well known to be a tricky passage, especially so with a strong tide. Narrow, it is only about a third of a mile across. In it are dangerous obstructions like the aptly named Bitch, and the Horse which shows only at low water. Was this a belated attempt by the owners to account for the loss of their ship in embarrassing circumstances or had the company been forced by speculation to admit the full story?

Fortunately, the 1837 edition of the Admiralty chart, surveyed by Lieut. H. M. Denham, R.N., is helpful for it marks the rock on which the *Albion* struck the year before. It is called the Crab and is so positioned on the exit to the Sound that, under the conditions existing at the time, it would seem only extreme carelessness or a sudden mishap like the one already described could have brought the *Albion* to grief there.

The spot where the *Albion* was beached is still marked by fragments which can be seen clearly at low tide. Denham's chart

13. Wreck of the *Albion*: photograph. On the horizon is Broad Sound between the two islands where the *Queen* came to grief.

marks the point where she was 'run ashore'. This short stretch of sand, divided from the main part of Marloes Sands by a barrier of rocks, the sort which you have to scramble over, and which leads to Gateholm Island, is now called by some Albion Sands.

The story also has its place in a local legend which recalls a time when there was pork galore.

3. The *Killarney*

[Built at Bristol 1830.
No. 28, 17 April 1830.
273 tons; length 118′; breadth (above) 30′3″; height 6′9″; 2 decks; 3 masts; ship rig; square stern; quarter galleries; bust head.]

Farr: Records of Bristol Ships: B.R.S. vol. XV.

The Irish route between Cork and Bristol was notoriously difficult in winter. It involved crossing that part of the Atlantic Ocean now called the Celtic Sea. Out of Cork, vessels met with the heavy rolling of the Ocean. And the rolling continued to the entrance of the Bristol Channel where vessels 'often met with a sea as bad, or worse, occasioned by the great strength of the tides.'

It was the effort of the steam packets to keep to advertised sailing times even in severe winter weather that was their greatest attraction to passengers. However, the expectations that a fixed timetable aroused in passengers made the captain's lonely decision, to sail or not to sail, more difficult. It was especially so from the shelter and safety of a harbour. Often a false start was necessary for the captain to test the conditions and give his passengers a taste of them.

George Bailey was well used to his responsibilities as a master on the Irish routes. Of all the masters of the Bristol General Steam Navigation Company's steamers none was more experienced than George Bailey. He had been a master in steamers almost eleven years. His value to the company was such that it was he who was entrusted with the special responsibility of introducing in turn the *City of Bristol*, *Killarney*, and *Osprey* into service. Only a matter of months previously he had had the shattering experience of losing his ship, the *Albion*, on the Pembrokeshire coast as already recounted, when his quick action in beaching her avoided the loss of a single life.

Now he was master of the *Killarney*, a ship worth £20,000, it was said. He had been with her for about five months, since her return to service after an extensive refit with new boilers, new coppering and engines overhauled, costing in all £5,000.

The *Killarney* had arrived on the Wednesday at Cork. She had taken on board, in the aft hold, a cargo consisting of flour, butter, bacon and leather, amounting in all to about 80 to 90 tons deadweight, less than half her capacity which was about 200 tons apart from her coals. But it was pigs that were her principal cargo. According to the captain there were about 650 pigs on board; 250 of them in the forehold and the rest on deck packed tight. Of the pigs 200 belonged to Michael Murphy, who had recently lost a cargo of pigs bound for London; 180 belonged to Messrs. Adams of Blackpool; and 70 to a woman called Sullivan.

Having taken on her passengers George Bailey made the decision to sail from Cork harbour at nine in the morning of Friday, 19 January, 1838, in accordance with his timetable.

The *Killarney* was about fifty yards off Penrose Quay, when the last passenger, Baron Spolasco, arrived. He was taken out in a rowing boat.

It had not been an easy decision for Captain Bailey. The weather was wintry with frost and snow. The wind was from the south-east and, in the reported words of the mate, 'blowing a fresh gale', but in his judgment not too hard to venture to sea.

Soon the *Killarney* was progressing, the mate estimated, at 6 to 6½ knots. However, on reaching Power Head, 'the sea was so bad, and the squalls increased so much, that the vessel put back.' She was not damaged, but the captain had decided on caution.

The *Killarney* reached the shelter of Cove about half-past one in the afternoon.

It was a disconcerting start for the passengers. One of them Richard Callaghan, brother to the M.P. for Cork, sensing 'a boisterous tedious voyage', disembarked there and then taking his luggage with him to Thomas's Hotel. Another, Lieut. Nicholay, son of Maj. Gen. Sir W. Nicholay, the Governor of the Mauritius, who was with the 99th Regiment stationed at Fermoy, decided to leave the ship and dine with his fellow officers at the fortress on Spike Island and return later in time to sail.

There were other young men on board. Two of them, John Collis of Castlecook, aged about 18, and Thomas Foster of Ballymaloo were going to England to be trained by Richard Beamish as engineers. And there was John Weldy, aged 25, the son of Capt. W. H. Weldy of Dowry Parade, Hotwells, Bristol, who had been making voyages to and fro between Bristol and Cork to gain experience in navigation in steamships. He was hoping to join the *Great Western*, which was at the time being got into shape to make her maiden voyage to New York in just under three months time. He wanted to be a navigating officer on her.

From Cork there was Mr. Robert Lawe, an 'extensive' coal merchant, travelling with his wife. Mr. Maurice Morrisy, a tanner of Mallow Lane, who was travelling to Bristol, with the intention of going on to London for goods. His wife was accompanying him and, it was said, carrying 180 sovereigns stitched between the lining of her stays.

Also on board was a friend of the captain's, called Collins, who was lame. He had arrived on the *Killarney* on the Wednesday and was making the return journey. Then there were Mr. C. Byrne from Tralee, he was making his way to London to appear as an important witness for the defence of Mr. Bateman in the case of the disputed Parliamentary election for the borough of Tralee; Mary Leary, also from Tralee, going to England 'to look for a situation'; James Evans, a shoemaker from the Marsh; Mr. J. M'Carthy from Kerry; Ellen Donovan of Dongourney, a stewardess on packet steamers, who was going to Bristol to join the *Herald*; and a 'pig boy' for Messrs. Adams. The Kerry Post reported that William Meredith of Rock Street was also on board.

In addition there were up to four other pig men. The most colourful of the passengers was undoubtedly Baron Spolasco. A literate man, who claimed foreign honours and medical degrees, he was going to England to meet, as he said with suitable mystery, 'the agent of a High Personage on a difficult surgical case'. He intended to practise in Bristol.

Spolasco had with him his young son Robert, aged $8\frac{1}{2}$, two large dogs and the 'chemical works, prescriptions, and receipts' of his profession. His books, 'several hundred volumes of the latest and best editions of surgical and medical works', and his surgical instruments, packed in fifty cases, were valued at £300. Also on board were his gig, household furniture, and several trunks of jewellery.

Arriving late he had to leave behind his carriage and decided that his English maid should accompany it by steamer on the following Tuesday. Spolasco had paid off his Irish maidservants.

For this passage he had paid altogether £5 12s..

The *Killarney* had lain at anchor at Cove for about three hours.

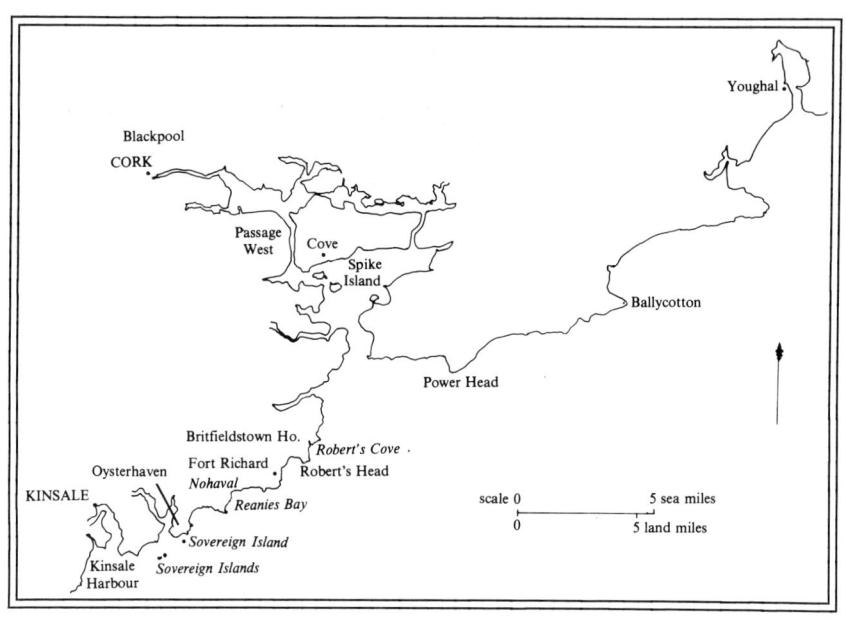

Map 5: Cork and the coast where the *Killarney* was in difficulties.

During this time, as a precaution, Capt. Bailey had ordered a further three tons of coal to be moved from the hold to the engine-room, fearing that the wind would make the passage longer than usual.

About half-past four Captain Bailey said to George Rowles, the mate, that as the wind was 'lulling fast', it would be a fine night and they had better get under way. Others later gave the opinion that the weather had 'in no way moderated'.

However, she sailed a second time.

Any misgivings that the passengers might have had about starting again remained with them below deck. What members of the crew regarded as reasonable weather, some of the passengers felt a good deal less sanguine about.

If Spolasco was surprised to hear the engines start up a second time, he was soon to become extremely disquieted.

'Shortly after we got out of Cork harbour (the second time)', he is reported as saying, 'the ship was very troublesome; my boy got very sick, and was put to bed, and the other passengers retired to their berths also.'

Spolasco's account continues:

'I lay on one of the sofas in the cabin, having no inclination to undress under the circumstances of the storm. I put on my cap lay down and went to sleep.

'I slumbered on the sofa till about 12 o'clock, and then went to my berth but did not undress at the time, the ship heaving dreadfully, and all the furniture which was not fastened to the floor was heaved about the room.

'It was about 2 o'clock in the morning on the Saturday that Ward, the ship's steward, went below. Conditions had worsened to a frightening extent. "Gentlemen," he said, "for God's sake, get up and dress, the ship is filling and we shall all be lost!"'

As the passengers stuck their heads out of their berths, they saw water swilling about the cabin. Apparently, water had rushed in through the aperture of the water closet, and under the closet door to the cabin. Spolasco had to pick his son's clothes out of the water before he could dress him.

More water was pouring through a deadlight which was in direct line to the gentlemen's cabin. It had been impossible to make this particular deadlight secure. And so in the heavy seas the water crashed through the glass.

The steward brought down the ship's carpenter to fix the deadlight, which was a wooden shutter about $2\frac{1}{2}$ feet square for keeping the sea from coming in through the porthole. He made several attempts to secure it with a mattress and board, but each time the sea burst through. The stewardess and her boy assistant did their best, 'sopping it up with mops'.

Spolasco himself was soaked trying to stop the water entering the cabin. Leaving his son below, he went up on deck to find out what was happening. There he found the engine had been stopped for some time. He noticed that there was no sail up either; and the ship was surrounded by a thick mist. Spolasco asked one of the passengers where they were. By his reply the passenger gave the impression that nobody knew where they were.

On the quarter-deck was Capt. Bailey. He had been there all the time save for a tea-break lasting twenty minutes.

Capt. Bailey estimated that they were about thirty-six miles south-east of Power Head, when the engineer came up and told him that there was a great deal of water in the vessel and that the engines would soon stop.

The mate in his reported evidence said they were thirty-five miles from Power Head with the wind blowing from due South-

East. He reckoned they were abreast of Youghal and Dungarvon. However, although he had been at sea for twenty-five years, he did not know navigation, but could do only the reckoning.

The captain did not go down to the engine-room to see what needed to be done; he had plenty to do on deck.

In fact, water was getting into the engine-room in some quantity, making it difficult for the men to serve the boilers.

William Hancock, a mariner from Bristol, who had been on sea for twelve years, was working his passage in the engine-room. He said that it was not the water that stopped the engines, but rather the water preventing the men from keeping the fires going. The water was not deep enough to swim in, but it was above his knees when the vessel rolled.

The boilers were placed on sleepers which put the boilers about eighteen inches or two feet above the ship's timbers. The men seeing to the fires moved about on a platform resting on the ship's timbers. The platform was lifted up by the water rising up underneath it. The men could not secure it and consequently they could not replenish the fires. To increase their difficulties the coal had become wet.

To use Spolasco's words, 'All was confusion, darkness and despair. Some of the passengers and crew spent the remainder of the night at the pumps. No one could keep his or her feet.'

The *Killarney* was in a very serious situation. However, for just such an emergency paddle-steamers were equipped with a set of sails.

Capt. Bailey decided to wear the ship round westwards to keep her head off shore and to prevent her drifting shorewards. In this attempt the storm was such that the staysail split. He ordered the trysail to be put up. With the wind there was the danger of the sails being torn to shreds. The captain was having the greatest difficulty in manoeuvring the *Killarney*.

His task was being made even harder by the problems being presented by his cargo of pigs. The 250 or so in the forehold had been stowed with the hatches open to give them air. The remaining 400 or so on deck were tightly penned in between the engine grating and the paddle-boxes. 'The deck was full of them, so much so that five more could not have been held there.'

Sometime after 2 a.m. with the storm taking control of events, heavy seas swept across the deck dislodging the pig planks. The pigs now unpenned were thrust to leeward, and the *Killarney* herself was thrust onto her lee beam. Capt. Bailey deeming it essential to correct the balance of his ship ordered the pigs to be pushed overboard.

This was no easy task. The deck was slippery and at a steep incline with the vessel listing at a sharp angle. To move about people had to crawl on hands and knees. Moreover, the 'pigs clung to the vessel as if they were destined to her destruction.'

Nevertheless, despite these difficulties in the storm and the darkness, about half the pigs were driven overboard. The ship thus lightened righted herself.

But matters below continued desperate with the water. All efforts were concentrated on pumping it out. The pumping and baling with buckets would seem to have stabilised the water level for a time. Even so, eventually all the pumps failed save one. It seems they had become choked by sucking in small coal.

Since about 2 a.m. the crew and some passengers had been hard at work at the pumps and baling under dreadful conditions. Soaked through and unable to maintain a footing on the slippery deck with the ship rolling, they crept along; just to keep on deck was immensely difficult. In this struggle the detail of time seemed irrelevant.

It was Saturday. Things continued in this way until the afternoon, when the captain ordered steam to be got up. The mate, in his account:

'went down about one o'clock to the engine-room to try and get the steam up, and succeeded for some time, say half an hour, by means of burning wood, but the cold water coming in under the boilers they were chilled . . .

'The wheels made some motion, and the engines plied, which could they have kept up for half an hour, would have brought them into Cove harbour.'

While the boilers were failing below, the captain made a last attempt to use sail. The jib was hoisted only to be blown away.

George Rowles, the mate, as reported, saw the situation like this:

'The vessel was unmanageable and the fog very dense; their object then was to keep off the shore; they were expecting the weather to get better; the sails were blown away and none to replace them.

'They were drifting on till near two o'clock on Saturday afternoon, the wind blowing very heavily; they could see the breakers on the rocks then, but no headlands; if they could make out the headlands they would know where they were...'

According to Spolasco it was Nicholay who first spotted land. Some said it was one place and some another. No one really knew what the captain thought. He had been on deck all night and much of the previous day. Some said it was Kinsale, others Cove.

Rowles, the mate, again:

'They were about one mile from the breakers, and were drifting dead down the shore; they endeavoured to sound by the hand line, but could not get any soundings; the water in the vessel was still increasing; all hands were baling ...'

When the fog cleared, the first land they positively identified was the Sovereign Islands. It now became clear just how far west they had drifted. The vessel had drifted to the west of its starting point, and here the coast was unfamiliar to Captain Bailey.

One of the passengers suggested to the captain that they make for shelter in Roberts's Cove. To get into the cove meant wearing the ship round. But she was within a mile of the breakers. Even if the captain had control of her, which he had not, there was not room enough to wear her round, for in so doing she would have needed to run a mile.

However, the captain had managed somehow to get his ship before the wind, in the direction of Roberts's Cove, when a tremendous sea broke over the stern. It carried with it the taffrail, the breakwater, the companion and the binnacle.

John Price and James Attwell, seamen, who were at the wheel, saved themselves by grabbing at the rigging. Not so fortunate were those steerage passengers who were standing at the funnel. They were swept away along with the bulwarks which should have protected them. The remaining pigs were also washed away.

The wind was continuing hard. The captain desperate to control his ship, dropped the larboard bower anchor. The vessel was now about a quarter of a mile from the shore and was drifting uncontrollably towards the rocks.

The anchor, it seems acted like a brake for long enough to check the vessel. She swung round avoiding a rock on which, it seemed, they would all have perished.

Then, by a slice of good fortune, the anchor broke in both flukes. The mate, on reflection, thought that if the anchor had held, the bows would have been torn out, or she would have foundered.

Below, in the ladies' cabin, was Mrs. Law. When things were looking bad before midnight she had changed from her night attire and put on a black silk gown. To Spolasco this indicated 'a wonderfully great degree of self possession, and calm deliberation'. Now she had assembled round her some of the passengers and, clasping her husband's hand, she raised her voice in prayer, and encouraged any sailors who looked in not to be afraid, and put their trust in God.

But the time of supplication was soon over. With the vessel drifting inevitably towards the rocks, the steward went below to call all the passengers on deck.

As Spolasco remembered it:

'The seas at this moment were heavens high, and the storm dreadfully terrific; we saw, in a few, moments, we must all perish. I grasped my child with one arm and held on with the other by the companion; the ship all this while nearing the rocks on her beam ends; she was almost perpendicular. It was now that horror was depicted in every countenance; the dreadful crisis was approaching.'

Lieut. Nicholay had prepared himself. On the advice of a sailor he had stripped off to his trousers to be ready to swim if necessary.

While the passengers made their way up, a sea passed over the ship. And when Mr. Lawe and Nicholay stepped onto the quarter-deck a wave crashed on to the deck. Lawe was dashed against the paddle-box and swept overboard. Nicholay was twirled around several times then swept into the sea. Riding on top of a mountainous wave, he disappeared.

Rope, spars and splinters fell on the deck. John Weldy, a few seconds before, had said, "Spolasco, have hopes, there is a chance for us yet." Then he like the others was swept into the sea.

Spolasco and his son were swept across the deck. Entangled in the debris they were saved by the bulwarks.

It was about 4.30 p.m. on the Saturday that the *Killarney* struck the Rennies, about two miles west of Roberts's Cove, described at the time as a chain of black, craggy rocks separated from each other by deep chasms into which the sea pours foaming. She struck the last of these rocks, the one nearest the shore.

Collis recalled that all of them were on the deck at that

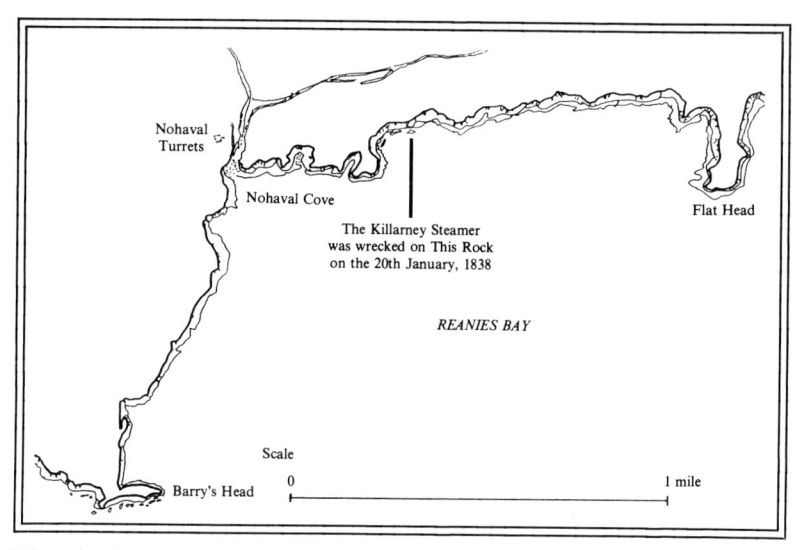

Map 6: The Rennies on which the *Killarney* was wrecked [based on the Ordnance Survey by permission of the Eire Government permit no 5736]. A survey of the coast was made first in 1841 by the Ordnance Survey. The rock came to be named on large scale O.S. maps 'Killarney Rock': though it is referred to generally as the Rennies, or, by some Rainey Rock.

moment, save Mrs. Lawe and the stewardess. Collis himself made for the stern and grabbed hard to the bulwarks.

The vessel hit first an outside rock where she broke her tiller chain; then she drifted to the last rock. Here she struck again. She moved backwards and forwards in rhythm with the sea, striking the rock each time. The passengers and crew timed their escape with the movement of the ship.

Spolasco described his escape thus:

'I got to that part of the stern nearest the rock; it was a jump of about four feet to the rock; half who had attempted to reach, or, who on reaching had not held firmly on, or gained a footing, fell into the sea. I saw poor Ward,' [he was the steward], 'go overboard in a jump, and saw the sea take him away . . .

'I shouted to those on the rock – "I am going to throw my child on the rock, for God's sake save him." They heeded me not, for they were looking to themselves, as everyman was in danger of being washed off.

'I gathered up the child and pitched him on the rock. The nerve I was obliged to command, and the desperate effort I had used, had the effect of nearly flinging me overboard. My child was landed on the rock . . .

'I had then to wait the lapse of several waves, which brought and took the ship from the rock – at length I seized an interval while a wave receded, and sprang forward and saved myself, getting hold of the crag and the sea washing over me.

'I scrambled up the rock where only the spray could reach me, taking with me my dear little boy.'

Having settled his son, Spolasco then went to give what aid he could, giving his hand to several.

Capt. Bailey, helped by the mate and the second steward, saw the first people on to the rock. Two or three people claimed to have helped Mrs. Lawe. Spolasco said he helped her on to the rock, but after a few minutes she slipped and was washed back into the sea.

It was observed that a woman, thought to be Maria Hayes, the stewardess, and a sailor were the last to leave the vessel. The sailor was seen carrying her in his arms apparently senseless. He jumped for the rock holding the woman under one arm. The rock was shelving with barely a toehold, and the sailor had only the fingers of one hand to gain a hold for both of them. He gained no hold, and the two of them fell back into the sea.

With Robert, Spolasco climbed the rock to find a higher position. This was no place for a child. And when Robert got up and moved away from his father's side, he stumbled and fell off the rock into the sea and was drowned.

Desperate, Spolasco with Collis, Foster, a woman and one of the engineers nearby spent the night holding on by fingers and toes, without rest, their backs towards the open sea, which was beating on to them.

The rock was made of a soft substance liable to crumble in the hand. It offered uneasy perches for the survivors. Sleep was a deadly danger in these circumstances, and they came to nudging and encouraging each other to keep awake.

Thirst added to their discomfort. There was spray and rain brought by the wind. The sailors used their sou'westers to catch the rain. Mary Leary, who drank the sea water, found that it greatly increased her thirst. Some ate the seaweed. Spolasco, who had eaten nothing since taking dinner at 4 or 5 o'clock on the Friday, took what little seaweed and salt water he could find.

There were those, who thinking that they might have to swim,

14. *The wreck of the steamer* Killarney *of Bristol on a rock at Renny Bay co. Cork*: lithograph, Jno. Unkles, 1838 (courtesy of Bristol Museums & Art Gallery).

had taken off their shoes or boots and discarded them. Some had discarded their soaking wet coats, not realising how much they might need them. Perhaps the worst off in this respect were Mary Leary, who was wearing only a nightdress and had a small handkerchief, and Thomas Foster.

Foster, working through the night baling water, had become soaked through. He was below in the cabin changing when all the passengers were ordered on deck. He had only a shirt and waistcoat for protection.

Collis, who was next to Foster on the rock, gave him a muffler, which he tied round his waist, and a pocket handkerchief, which Collis helped him to tie round his head.

It was very cold in the darkness and it rained almost incessantly. Collis and Foster stood through the night, their toes thrust into holes in the rock, and holding on with their hands. At daybreak Collis found that Foster had succumbed to the cold. Later it was discovered that three seamen and both of the engineers had died, one where he sat astride the rock.

The chief hope of those on the rock during that dreadful January night was that when day came and the tide went out they would be able to walk to safety.

Imagine their disappointment when they woke to see that a dangerous sea lay between them and the shore. 'It was,' as Spolasco put it, 'the hope of saving ourselves next morning that enabled us to keep our hold the first night.'

Local people, about twenty of them, had been spotted by the crew from the rock. They did not respond to the shouts which could not reach them against the wind. But after a time they were seen to clamber down the cliff face and carry off some of the pigs that had been washed ashore. The mate said that they had heard during the night people picking away at the wreck.

On the Sunday morning, early, the country people appeared again. To Spolasco there seemed to be several hundreds of them carrying away pieces of wreckage. He stood up and shouted to them offering his purse, and all that he possessed if they would come to help them. But in the storm his words were blown away.

However, Edward Galwey of Fort Richard, who had sent a message to the packet agent at Cork telling him of the disaster, on his own initiative led a band of rescuers to the clifftop among them Knowles, and Conway and Robinson of the St. George Packet Company. And it was Galway himself who took great risk in descending the sloping edge of the cliff to wave encouragement to those on the rock far below.

The rock, on which the survivors were, lay between two promontories, but closest to a very steep cliff of, it was thought, 250 ft. or more. It lay so close in that the rescuers, on the top of the cliff, would have had to stand very close to the edge to have a good view of it.

The rescuers proceeded with various attempts to establish a line to the rock. Some of the gentry, attached to ropes, stood near the edge and threw stones with lines tied to them. When that failed they used slings, again without success. Then ducks were tried with lines attached to their legs. One duck reached the rock but no one could catch it.

Galwey was seen to produce a musket. By means of a coiled line attached to a musket ball, it was hoped that the musket shot would carry the line to the rock. It did not.

But the rescuers were men of resource. Mr. Edward Hull, brother to the officer of the coastguard at Roberts's Cove, suggested using a very long rope. The idea was to secure the end of the rope to one promontory and then take it along the cliff to the other. There the rope was to be brought into line over the rock and the end secured.

This they did. And to their delight, they saw the "belly" of the line droop nicely over the rock. Down this line, using another trip line, they were able now to work a dependent rope with a weight attached. At last contact was established.

The rescuers could see a man fixing himself to the dependent rope. But in the excitement, a pig boy anxious to take his chance clung to the rope too. The rope was not strong enough for both of them. The two were lost as they were being hauled through the water by the trip line.

This was a terrible disappointment after so many others. But it was dark by this time and so the rescuers decided to abandon any further efforts that day.

The evening was fine, but the wind was blowing strong, as the survivors looked to spending another night on the rock.

Collis found himself a split in the rock about 2 feet wide. He and another squeezed themselves into it for warmth. The night turned out to be calmer and not so cold.

When Monday morning arrived, there was great activity on the way to the wreck. Those who sought to give help were in covered

15. *Captain Manby's mortar lifeline*: engraving, S. Sly, 1843 (by kind permission of The Illustrated London News Picture Library).

cars or on horseback. While some country people, leaving the business of rescue to the gentry, the coastguard and their helpers, were already on their way back home. Some were carrying planks and pieces of oak that required the strength of three or four men.

Hundreds of people, it seems, men and women, were thus occupied risking the perilous path to this customarily deserted shore, climbing dangerously back up the cliffs with their gains.

Meanwhile, Galwey was early on the clifftop. With him were Hull and others, including the coastguard commanded by Capt. Irving and Mr. Charlesson from Oyster Haven with Capt. Manby's Life Preserving Apparatus from Kinsale.

They started by using Manby's technique, attaching a rope to a cannon ball putting it in a small howitzer and shooting it across the rock. But it did not work.

So they reverted to Hull's already tested method with the ropes. Having established a line, they used Manby's equipment. A hawser, that is a much stronger rope, was sent out to the rock to make a more secure link, and then they slid a basket along it. In it there were two loaves of bread, some wine and spirits, and a note from Conway, the packet agent, explaining how the ropes were to be used.

The captain shared out the supplies; Mary Leary, the only

woman, had hers first. Collis put a piece of bread in his mouth, but could not move his jaws. It took a glass of whiskey to loosen them.

Now after all the setbacks everything went well. A cot with iron grummets was run along the hawser from the cliff to the rock, and one by one the survivors were drawn to safety. Collis scrambled up the slippery cliff path and was carried the last part on the back of Charles Newenham to the nearest house. The last to leave was George Rowles, who, it was noted, had done most of the work getting the survivors off the rock. This was about half-past one on the Monday afternoon, roughly two and a half days from the time when things started to go badly wrong.

Of the passengers, three only had survived; Mary Leary, Baron Spolasco and John Collis. Captain Bailey and the mate, George Rowles, survived; and so did Michael Sheehan, 2nd Steward, Charles Goodland, William Hancock, John Champion, William Paterson, James Halnan, and George Porter, coal trimmer. James Mason, carpenter, died soon after landing.

Of the ship only the boilers were to be seen.

Among the rescuers were some women. Lady Roberts was singled out as a heroine. She was, it seems, on the clifftop keeping vigil with the rescuers from the beginning. She was on hand with her servants, armed with blankets, clothes and food ready for the survivors as they were landed.

Conway, the packet agent, was overwhelmed by this vision of delight: 'It was really astonishing to see this young and lovely woman buffeting one of the greatest storms I have witnessed . . .'

Spolasco for his part found a suitable quotation:
'O Woman! in the hour of deepest wo,
When all around to torture us combine,
'Tis then thy tender kindness most we know,
Thy heart angelic and thy feelings fine!'

Conway also found time to write another letter to the press acknowledging the help given by the country people who had been criticised in some quarters for their lack of humanity. He praised them for 'opening their doors to receive the poor sufferers as they were landed, lighting fires and getting dry straw to keep them warm.' Particularly he mentioned Macarthy, a carpenter, for his 'brave and intrepid conduct'. He had offered to swim to the wreck with a rope tied round him. However, as a husband and the father of eight children, he was dissuaded from doing so.

16. *The wreck of the steamer* Killarney *of Bristol . . . showing the scene of the disaster . . . & the mode of rescue*: lithograph, Jno. Unkles, 1838 (courtesy of Bristol Museums & Art Gallery). Unlike others which clearly were not, it is claimed that this sketch was made on the spot. It would seem to be a very fair representation.

Capt. Irving's report to the Inspector General of the Coastguard was leaked to the press. Its self-applauding note was roundly criticised in the Cork Southern Reporter, '. . . it appears selfishly silent, as to the aid and exertions freely, and generously, and humanely contributed by the neighbouring gentry – and let us not forget the active benevolence of the ladies . . .'

The survivors were given shelter locally and were visited daily by a doctor, William M'Dermott, with whom Spolasco stayed. Collis stayed at Lady Roberts'; Capt. Bailey at the Water Guard station; Mary Leary, Rowles, and two of the crew at Mr. Galwey's; three sailors with Capt. Welland; two with the Rev. Mr. O'Flynn; and Sheehan with a poor man at Bally-feard. Some of them were warned that they would have to give evidence at an inquest.

At the end of the week, ten of the survivors were taken to the Southern Infirmary at Cork for a check-up. And after an overnight stay all but four were discharged. Detained were George Porter, who had ulcerated knees from kneeling so long on the rock; Mary Leary, who suffered from inflammation of the legs and had an injured toe; George Price, whose jaw was injured when he was struck by a wheel in the engine-room, he could still eat only bread soaked in milk; and Michael Sheehan, who had seriously aggravated the condition of his legs and feet by soaking them in water that was too warm.

For Price, Sheehan and their captain this was their second shipwreck in nine months. They had been together on the *Albion*.

In the days before the inquest there were rumours flying about. Some of these were published by the Cork Constitution as an example of the 'plunder and fiendish cruelty of the peasantry'. One rumour alleged that the rings were cut off Mrs. Morrisy's fingers; another that the peasantry had cut the rope to the rock during the Sunday night.

These unsubstantiated allegations against the country people were refuted in the strongest terms by the Cork Southern Reporter, which then proceeded with gusto to make political points of its own. It accused the Tory, or Orange, Press of advocating 'the domination of a small minority of the Population and the political inferiority and degradation of the great majority . . . the Irish Tory has no patriotism, no love of country.' He has, it went on, a 'hostile disposition to, if not an actual hatred of, the great body of his countrymen.'

With regard to the story of the wreck itself, readers in Cork and Bristol were exceptionally well informed by detailed reports in the press and, uniquely, by dramatic lithographic engravings which were made in Cork and first used by the newspapers there. Bristol editors were much impressed. The Bristol Mirror, for example, obtained a print from the proprietors of the Cork Constitution and had it re-engraved for printing in its own paper. The printed copies of the lithograph which appeared in the newspapers were also available for purchase separately.

The inquest on the body of Maurice Morrisy occupied five full days. The jury consisted of 'individuals engaged in the butter trade, and other respectable persons.'

The mayor and sheriffs attended the opening in the Court House. The coroner was Henry Hardy, Esq.; Mr. Scanell represented the friends of the deceased; and Mr. Parker acted for the company. Mr. Conway, the St. George Steam Packet Company agent, who was also the Bristol company's agent in Cork, represented the company.

There were fourteen jurymen listed: Bernard Sheehan, Timothy Haly, Michael Cox, Jeremiah Corbett, James Russell, Jeremiah Buckley, John Buckley, William Carrol, John Hayes, John Meade, Bartholomew Cotter, Daniel Buckley, John Hogan and John Hallnane.

The seamen who were called to give evidence during the inquest were supportive of their captain, both as a character and for the way he handled things during the voyage.

Early in the proceedings an attempt was made to unsettle the evidence of William Hancock, the first seaman to give evidence.
Mr. Scanell (for the deceased): 'Who gave you that new jacket you have on?'
Mr. Conway (the company agent): 'It was I who gave it him because he was naked.'
Mr. Parker (supporting Conway): 'I submit to you, Mr. Coroner, whether this question, which carries an imputation of bribery with it, is one which should be put in the hearing of this jury?'
Mr. Scanell: 'It is perfectly fair. The witness gives his evidence favourably for the one side, and reluctantly on the other. I have therefore the right to assume he is not giving his evidence fairly.'
The Coroner: 'I don't go as far as that. However the jury is

composed of intelligent men, and they can appreciate his evidence.'

As the inquest proceeded, a certain lack of ease manifested itself from time to time.

A group of about a dozen country gentlemen entered the court room in the middle of the proceedings on the first day. Having disturbed the court in the manner of their entry, one of them Sir Thomas Roberts of Britfieldstown House, a magistrate and the husband of the heroine, further interrupted the proceedings with a question of his own quite irrelevant to the matter in hand.

This was no routine inquest. The public interest was involved, the packet company, and so were the local gentry. This in turn put pressure on the coroner, the jury and the witnesses.

Careful questioning failed to discover precisely how such a vast amount of water entered the ship.

Mr. Parker, solicitor for the company, was anxious to establish the captain's character, and his conduct in the crisis.

His pressing questions proved tiresome to Collis, the apprentice engineer. Collis, whose entry into the court supported by three or four friends had aroused sympathy among the spectators, now excited admiration. In answer to the question, "What was the captain doing on Friday night?"

"For aught I know," Collis replied, "the captain might have spent the whole of Friday night in his bed. I cannot say for certain where he spent the night. He might have been asleep on top of one of the paddle-boxes for aught I know . . ." Laughter in court.

But when on the second day the company's solicitor insinuated that some members of the jury had disregarded the rules of behaviour by talking to witnesses or members of the public, there was no laughter. Several jurymen stood up in court and made it plain 'in very warm terms to the learned solicitor' that they had been grossly insulted.

George Rowles, the first mate, also found some of the questions trying:

'A juror: Why did you not get into Youghal?

Rowles: if we had cats' eyes we might.'

In answer to a further question:

'Rowles: We could not clear the Soverign Islands in order to get into Kinsale. If you were mounted on a blood mare, with both her front legs broken, I don't think you could manage her very well.'

Despite the testiness, the inquest did not turn into a witch hunt.

No one took advantage of Captain Bailey's humiliating position.

For Spolasco's evidence, the court went to his lodgings in King Street. He had been shattered by the experience. The court was assembled around his bed from which he gave evidence. He was placid for the most part, and gave evidence in an extremely coherent manner.

During his evidence, which occupied the court for a whole day, it was clear that Spolasco, although unhappy about the *Killarney* setting sail the second time, felt that it was the pigs that were the key to the disaster.

'I said with the others, "Why are not the pigs thrown overboard?" I never sailed but once where pigs were on board, and I shall never go again if I can help it.

'. . . thirty-one human beings were sacrificed for the pigs . . . with our eyes open we were lost by the pigs.'

The most critical thing Spolasco said about the captain was, 'I think the captain was too tenacious of the lives of the pigs.'

The jury in its verdict found that Captain Bailey had done his utmost to preserve his vessel and the lives of those on board. It was unhappy that he did not go below to find out for himself why the fires could not be kept going. Further, the jury was concerned about the pigs. It found that the great number of pigs on board 'tended in a great measure to increase the danger during the said gale of wind, and to accelerate her loss.'

Two recommendations followed:

that the 'proper authorities' be asked to make regulations for the export of pigs and cattle, 'so that the safety of the passengers and crew may not be endangered by them.'

that life boats and other proper machinery be kept on the coast by the Coastguard for use in the case of shipwrecks.

At a meeting held at the Commercial Rooms, under the chairmanship of the Rev. H. G. Walsh, curate of Clifton, local worthies, including the mayor, formed a committee to manage a relief fund. The directors of the Bristol General Steam Navigation Company gave £100 to the fund. There was a grand performance of sacred music from the oratorios in the parish church at Clifton. And at a benefit given at the Theatre Royal Mrs. Colman Pope spoke the verse written for the occasion, ending:

'Bristolians! Charity breathes no vain prayer
Within your walls – her proudest temple's there.
Oh! Let the spark which lit up Colston's heart

And Reynold's generous soul to yours impart
Some kindred ray to light the holy flame
Which sheds a halo round each sacred name! . . .'

When the fund came to be closed a few weeks later it stood at £1,390 8s. 6d., with some small expenses still outstanding.

The editor of the Bristol Mirror made weighty and well balanced observations. While not wishing 'to offer any check to that enterprising spirit which has rendered the nautical skill and naval superiority of this country a household word throughout the world . . .', he went on to question that the lives and property of those who embark in steam ships should 'for the sake of saving a few hours, or competing with rival establishments, or defying opposition' be 'brought into situations of extreme peril if not certain destruction . . .'

The directors of the company, taking this as being an imputation of their being reckless of life and property, claimed the right of reply.

The company assured all users of their ships 'that the instructions to all their Commanders of Vessels engaged in their service have been distinctly to delay their voyages on the occurrence of heavy gales and foul weather, at the fixed points of sailing, and generally to avoid risking life, ship and cargo for the sake of dispatch.'

The directors continued, 'the circumstance of their never insuring would, indeed, of itself be a sufficient guarantee against their wishing the Commanders of their Vessels to run unnecessary risks.'

And now to business. 'The *Killarney*', they went on, 'has been replaced by the *City of Bristol*, which vessel sailed yesterday for Cork, with an unusual number of passengers.'

The statement was signed by Peter Maze, C. L. Walker, Thomas Camplin, Frederick Ricketts, Thomas Cole, John Gilmore, Joseph Russell, George Lunell, and W. H. Marshall. The show must go on.

The editor of the Cork Southern Reporter sought to provide a helpful perspective which makes a fitting conclusion to this tragic episode.

'Everyone,' he wrote, 'who is in the habit of crossing from this country to England must count occasionally upon disagreeable and even perilous passages; but we think it tells well for the discretion and management of the steam vessels from this port, that the loss of the *Killarney* is the only one which has ever occurred, out of, or bound to it, since their establishment; and when it is considered they have made, upon a calculation, sixty thousand passages to and from English ports, however greatly to be deplored the one loss is – its singleness is at least a presumptive proof of good ships, good management in the direction, and competent skill in navigating them.'

4. The *City of Bristol*

[Built at Bristol 1828.
No. 13, 7 Mar. 1838.
210 tons; length 143'9"; breadth (above) 23'1"; depth 15'3"; main, quarter and forecastle decks; 2 masts; schooner rig; square stern; quarter galleries; scroll head; a steam vessel.]
Farr: Records of Bristol Ships: B.R.S. vol. XV.

From the time of her launch in 1827 the *City of Bristol* was well known among the wooden-hulled paddle-steamers that sailed out of Bristol bound for Ireland.

Built at the War Office Steam Packet's newly acquired yard at Hotwells, her engines were made in Bristol by Messrs. Winwood of Cheese Lane, St. Philip's. In fact she was the first steam packet wholly made in Bristol. Thus her proud name, the *City of Bristol*, has an entirely appropriate ring about it.

Originally she was built to sail between Bristol and Dublin. But at the time we are concerned with her, she was on the Bristol to Waterford run.

John Stacey, master of the *City of Bristol*, had been with her only about six weeks. He had joined her on her return to service after an extensive refit. The refit, at a reputed cost of £5,000, had included new boilers.

For Capt. Stacey, in his early fifties, and born at Pill, sailing out of Waterford was no new experience. He had been known in Waterford for 'full forty years' with the Bristol packets; first in sail then in steam. It was said that he was highly respected in Waterford by all who knew him.

When the *City of Bristol* left Waterford on Tuesday, 17 November, 1840, the cargo she carried was typical of the Southern Irish trade of the time: 575 barrels of oats; 113 barrels of barley; 2 tierces of lard; 120 flitches of bacon; 15 fine bullocks in the fore-hold; and 280 pigs penned in with planks on the deck. Apparently she could carry 320 pigs on deck, and 500 altogether with ease. Indeed, John Hyde, who had been master of her for some years, reckoned that once she had taken 800.

There were no cabin passengers. There were, however, a few deck passengers, perhaps five or six.

One was Thomas Henderson, a young man, of Patrick Street, Waterford. He was on his way to London to buy secondhand clothes. His family dealt in them. Another young man, named Walsh, came from Liverpool. He had arrived at Waterford recently, and, it was said, he was on his way back taking a roundabout route by way of Bristol. There was a woman passenger, nothing is known of her. The other deck passengers were men travelling with the cattle and pigs; 'pig men' or 'pig jobbers' as they were called. There were two or three of them. John Sullivan, the only one known by name, was in charge of the pigs.

The weather was moderate as the *City of Bristol* left Waterford on schedule at eight o'clock in the morning. At ten o'clock she went by Passage.

However, the weather soon deteriorated; a gale began blowing,

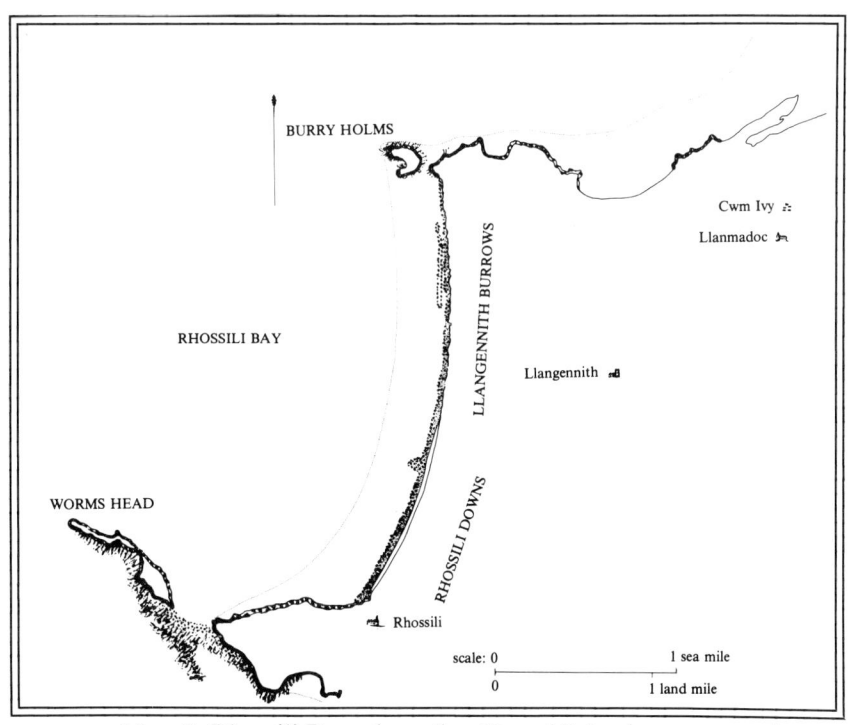

Map 7: Rhossili Bay where the *City of Bristol* ran aground.

making the seas frightening. Capt. Stacey decided to return for shelter. By four o'clock she was anchored in Duncannon Bay, three miles below Passage.

Some hours later, when the weather had abated, Capt. Stacey decided to continue. And so he put to sea a second time about an hour before midnight.

Nothing worthy of remark happened in the night, but the weather began to change as they approached the Pembrokeshire coast.

William Poole, seaman, continues the story:

'About six o'clock the following morning (Wednesday), when we were off the Smalls, it began to blow very hard, the wind being at the south-east. We saw St. Govan's Head about noon that day, and we did not see land again until we saw the Caldey Light, which was about a quarter to five o'clock on Wednesday evening.'

At this point Poole was at the helm, and he helped the captain to set Caldey. The weather was then very thick and hazy; it was dark and raining and the wind was blowing strong.

'The captain said he should anchor to the north of Worm's Head, for shelter during the night.'

Poole continued:

'About a quarter after six o'clock we observed land on our larboard quarter (Burry Holmes), and immediately afterwards land on our starboard (the Worm's Head).'

She was too close in to shore, and too far northward to benefit from the shelter offered by Worms Head.

Just before this, a man had been sent to fetch a lead line, but any anxieties the watch may have had did not reach below deck.

'We experienced no alarm whatever . . . We were all at tea but the watch.'

As for the *City of Bristol*, she was moving irrevocably to the rough edge of the sea where it was pounding on the Llangennith Sands in Rhossili Bay.

Then she struck . . .

As they felt her run on to the sands, everyone below ran up on deck.

The helm was put hard a-port. Thomas Anstice, the ship's carpenter, heard Capt. Stacey say, "Stop the engines!" and order the jib to be run up to keep her head out. Then he ordered the engines to be turned a-head and then the mainsail run up. But it was all to no avail.

The *City of Bristol* had taken now by the stern, her engines and sails were powerless to free her; and the force of the sea drove her further astern.

Then her head canted towards Burry Holmes, and she lay grounded broadside on to the full force of the waves.

The captain ordered the engines to be stopped and the sails taken down. And to warn the people on the land of their distress, he commanded blue lights to be got ready and fired off. Anstice could see a small light on the beach.

With the sea breaking over her very forcefully, Anstice was told by the captain to see if she was making any water. He found that she was bilged, that is she had sprung a leak, and was making a great deal of water.

Anstice recollected:

'the sea was rising worse and worse as the flood tide came on. The captain consulted with the crew about lowering the boats down but they said that the boats would not live a moment in such a sea.

'He then asked whether it was not possible to make a stage with the pig planks . . .

'I said that it was not possible to get at them, because the sea was breaking over her so, that no man could go forward. He desired me to open the gangway so that the pigs might get out. The sea then burst tremendously over us, and swept everything off the deck.

'. . . when all hopes of getting her off were given up, all the persons on board got on the quarter deck, except the female passenger who remained near the forecastle.

'About high water the vessel separated at the break of the quarter deck. Some of the persons in the meantime had gone forward.

'I remained on the quadrant near the wheel. The stewardess and a man named Stephen Turner [one of the firemen] were with me.'

Anstice helped lash the stewardess to the rails as she could not hold on. She was in a bad state, and, left alone, she untied the knot and went to join the others on the quarter deck.

Meanwhile Anstice and Turner positioned themselves on the mainmast. When the mainmast broke and fell into the body of the wreck, they were forced to seek refuge at the quadrant again. Shortly after, Turner was washed away. And Anstice saw a heavy sea sweep most of the people off the quarter deck; everything remaining was swept off by the following sea.

When the ship broke up Anstice was on the stern, which was being swept round and round with frightening speed. He chose his moment and swam for shore.

Soon Anstice was walking towards a fire burning on the shore; the people there took him to safety.

William Poole told of his experiences:

'... the vessel held together till nearly about high water (between twelve and one o'clock) that night ... we stayed by the vessel in the hope that she would hold together until the tide left her. We knew we were near the shore from hearing the people.'

Poole was standing in the forerigging with the captain, the mate and two seamen when the body of the ship started breaking into three parts. The mast fell taking them into the middle of the wreck. Poole found himself in the middle of the cross-trees half in and half out of the water. There was one man with him, but he saw nothing of the captain and the others.

He reached one of the paddle-boxes but was soon swept off. He grabbed what he thought was a plank of wood and a feather pillow and was swept with them to the shore.

It seems it was by this time about twelve o'clock in the morning, and bystanders on the shore rushed into the surf to bring Poole in.

He was taken by them, with broken ribs, badly bruised and unwell, to the inn in Llangennith. There he saw Thomas Anstice, the ship's carpenter. They were the only survivors.

In Bristol there was no particular anxiety on the Wednesday evening when the *City of Bristol* was scheduled to arrive on her passage from Waterford. The weather generally had been boisterous during the week; and it was assumed the weather had caused her to delay sailing.

But on the Thursday morning, there were vague rumours in the city that all was not well with the *City of Bristol*.

Eager for hard news among the rumours, a large crowd waited at Cumberland Basin. The people there knew that the Swansea packet was due and that she might have some news.

In fact it was the *County of Pembroke*, Capt. Henry Gerard, coming from Tenby, which arrived first bringing the devastating news. For the Bristol merchants who needed confirmation, there was a note from Swansea in the Commercial Rooms.

Just how devastating the news was for the shipping community of Bristol was soon made apparent.

Thirteen of the crew, it was said, including the captain, had been born in the village of Pill, that nursery of Bristol seafarers.

Felix Farley's Journal published a list of the crew:
Captain – John Stacey, leaving a wife and one daughter.
1st Mate – William Moore, leaving a wife and nine children, the eldest girl being about 15 years old.
2nd Mate – Richard Wright, his wife in her confinement with her first child.
Seamen – John Wright, unmarried; William Poole, saved; Joseph Nicholson, a wife; John Reed, unmarried: Terence O'Brien, a wife; James Stacey, unmarried.
1st Engineer – Donald Frazer, unmarried; 2nd Engineer, Charles Collier, a wife and seven children.
Firemen – James Hill and James Pinnel, each a wife and two children; Stephen Turner, a wife and four children.
Carpenter – Thomas Anstice, saved.
Coaltrimmers – Patrick Hayne, a wife and seven children; William Grace, a wife and three children.
2nd Steward – Robert Crump, a wife and one child.
Stewardess – Sarah Jordan, unmarried.
Cook – James Cromwell, a wife and four children.
Cabin boy – Thomas M'Cormack.

There are always difficulties with lists of this kind. And where there are obvious errors in the names they have been corrected. Thomas Anstice, for example, was also known as Thomas Hamlin. Two people are missing from this list. For Edward Braynes, a seaman, and Thomas Gotherick, 3rd steward, both of the *City of Bristol* are buried at Llangennith Church.

Counting these two it appears that twenty-one of the crew were drowned in addition to the five or six passengers.

A public meeting was held in the Commercial Rooms with Charles Ludlow Walker, Esq., in the chair. It had the object of establishing a committee to organise the subscription for the widows and orphans, which had already been opened.

The committee then went on to authorise that 'circulars be sent to the Public Bodies, Clergy, Ministers and Influential Individuals in the neighbourhood soliciting subscriptions.'

Subscriptions could made at the different banks, the Commercial Rooms, the Institution in Park Street and at the libraries in Clifton.

When the account was published in May, 1841, it was revealed that over £900 was raised. Each of the thirteen widows received £15 and thirty-four dependant children were given £14 each.

An inquest was held at the King's Head, Llangennith, landlord William Tucker, on Friday, 20 November. It was summoned by Charles Collins, the coroner. William Taylor was the foreman; with him were Francis Batcock, William Taylor, William Robert, David Lewis, John Clark, William Tucker, William Nicholas, John Taylor, George Richard, yet another William Taylor and William Richards.

William Poole and Thomas Anstice told their stories. The jury returned verdicts of accidental death on Capt. Stacey, Richard Wright, James Stacey, Edward Braynes, Thomas Gotherick, William Grace and an unknown male passenger.

Three days later the jury met to return similar verdicts on Charles Collier, John Reed, James Pinnel and another unknown male passenger.

In the ensuing days six more bodies, five men and a woman, were washed up. The coroner again held inquests. By this time Poole and Anstice had returned to Bristol, making the problem of identification impossible for all save one.

Mrs. Margaret Urquhart was staying in Llangennith in the hope of recovering her brother's body and taking it back to Bristol for burial. And so it fell to her to identify her brother, Donald Frazer, the ship's first engineer.

Nearly four weeks after the disaster, the schooner, *Shepherd*, soon after leaving harbour at Llanelli, took the body of a woman from the water. It was the stewardess, Sarah Jordan, and curiously on the finger of her left hand was a gold and diamond ring. A mourning ring, it bore the inscription 'Sarah Jordan, Obit. 1 April, 1840, æt. 52.'

From the beginning the *City of Bristol*'s owners, the Bristol General Steam Navigation Company, had kept a presence at Llangennith.

Silvanus Padley, long connected with the harbour at Swansea and with extensive commercial interests in the town, was, among other things, agent for the Bristol packet company at Swansea. He quickly took it upon himself to send written confirmation to Bristol. He said that he had engaged Capt. Edwards of the *Mountaineer* to ensure that the wreck and the remaining cargo were secured as far as possible.

In his anxiety to keep the company informed and, perhaps, to make his own position more secure, Padley wrote two letters to them on the same day. One letter was to be conveyed by the packet steamer *Bristol* and, in case that should be delayed, another was to be sent overland by mail coach. He awaited further instructions.

Also awaiting further instructions was George Holland of Cwm Ivy farm, Llanmadoc, Lloyd's agent for that part of the Gower coast. He wrote to say that he was making secure such of the cargo and the wreck as were on shore. Later he informed the company that 3 head of cattle and about 75 pigs had survived, and several bags of oats and meal were saved. The stock had been taken to his farm at Cwm Ivy nearby.

In due course, the company heard from Holland that he had sold all the drowned pigs and cattle that had been washed up on shore badly bruised.

The *City of Bristol* was lost during a bad patch of weather that stormy November. A few days before, the Bristol Gazette had reported there had been awful gales. Ships had been lost off Bideford, Whitby, Harwich and Lowestoft. A ship was driven ashore at Brighton and the docks at Portsmouth and Southampton had been damaged.

Bristol newspapers were reluctant to stir up controversy over the disaster. But the Gazette did carry a report suggesting that the captain of the *City of Bristol* was at fault in approaching the coast to seek shelter. Things had been manageable, it said, all were below having tea; but the moment she touched – disaster. It went on to concede, however, that darkness and the inclemency of the weather might have baffled the captain's calculations.

William Poole had put it differently, 'We must have made more way than the captain thought,' he said.

As usual storm and shipwreck captured the public's imagination. 'Paul', writing from York, suggested in the Bristol Mercury that there should be a weather house built with a barometer in a room 15 to 20 feet square. The barometer was to be placed in a window, so that it might be consulted from inside or outside the room. The object was to prevent captains taking to sea against discouraging readings of the barometer.

The Bristol Gazette carried a letter calling for a fund 'for the relief of mercantile seamen generally'. It was signed 'An old seaman'. He knew full well that between a few large catastrophies there lay many small disasters that went unnoticed by the public at large.

The directors of the Bristol General Steam Navigation Company had requested George Lunell, a leading one of their number, to go to the scene of the accident.

George Lunell, merchant, shipbuilder and shipowner, would appear to have been a man of presence and a generosity of spirit.

In a letter to Felix Farley's Journal he wrote:

'. . . on Saturday morning, I left Bristol by the Swansea mail, and before daylight on Sunday went from Swansea, in company with Capt. Edwards, of the *Mountaineer*, to Rhosilly Bay, where we arrived a few minutes before low water. The steam-chest and the upper part of the machinery only were visible, we could not get nearer than within 50 yards of them; they appeared to be in about 12 feet of water, and heavy surf was rolling over them. Detached pieces of the vessel were lying a considerable distance apart on the sands, and the entire Bay was covered with broken fragments of the wreck. We made arrangements with Mr. Holland, the Agent for Lloyd's, for the preservation of the property, and after I had been sometime on the beach, I had the gratification of being joined by my friend Mr. Claxton, who, after viewing the wreck, kindly accompanied me to the church at Llangennith, where the whole of the unfortunate sufferers who had been found had been deposited, and whose remains I was anxious to see, as I thought the knowledge that I had done so might afford some consolation to their afflicted relations.

'After this melancholy duty was performed, we repaired to the small inn, where the two survivors were staying, and I requested Capt. Claxton, being more conversant with nautical affairs than myself, to have the goodness to take their depositions, the particulars of which have been published.

'My principal object of writing the present is to afford myself the gratification publicly to return my best thanks to the Rev. C. Phillips, [in fact, the Rev. Samuel Phillips of Llangennith, who lived at Fairyhill], the clergyman of the parish, for his unceasing solicitude: he was daily with me some hours on the beach with the gentleman who officiates as his curate, and by their presence and influence contributed much to preserve that excellent order and good conduct, which was at all times

manifested. To T. Collins, Esq., coroner, and Mr. Holland, Agent for Lloyd's, I feel obliged by their kind and prompt attention; to the Churchwardens I am indebted for the regard with which they treated the remains of the sufferers; if indeed, instead of being strangers, they had been relatives, they could not have shown them more respect; and with gratitude I bear testimony to the honesty and high moral integrity of all the inhabitants of the neighbourhood; though every part of the bay was strewed with broken fragments, and continued so for six days and nights, though many of the people were poor, and fuel was scarce and dear, not the smallest particle was taken; but on Wednesday last, after disposing in small lots of all the timbers and planks that had come on shore, I told them they were welcome to what remained, and nothing could show more strongly that it had not been previously taken because not valued, than after thanking me, they immediately set about gathering it up, and in less than two hours scarcely a vestige was to be seen. From everyone I received sympathy and kindness, and the remembrance of the last few days will never occur to my recollection unaccompanied with a feeling of respect and gratitude towards the inhabitants of Llangennith and its neighbourhood . . .'
The letter was dated, 'Bristol, Nov. 27 1840'.

17. Wreck of the *City of Bristol*: photograph taken at low tide.

5. The *Queen*

[Built at Bristol, 1838.
No. 48, 29 Oct. 1838.
288 tons o.m.; 298 tons n.m.; length 150′; depth 14′8″; 1 deck; 2 masts; schooner rig; square stern; false galleries; woman bust head; propelled by steam; engine room 54′8″ long and 200 tons]
Farr; Records of Bristol Ships; B.R.S. vol. XV.

For reference see Maps 4 and 2

The *Queen*, named after the young Queen Victoria, was in the words of an observer, 'a very superb vessel'.

In October, 1842, she had had a new master Cornelius Charles Gardiner. Aged about 44, it was a good appointment for him, since he was Bristol born.

His previous appointment had been as master of the *Arabian*, 387 tons, an East Indiaman, registered and owned in Bristol by Messrs. W. D. & W. E. Acraman. His mastership lasted some 19 months and during that time he had made a voyage in her to Launceston in Van Dieman's Land, as Tasmania was called in those days, with stops at Calcutta and Batavia, before returning to London.

However, it was a different business altogether being master of an Irish steam packet.

The *Queen*, it has to be said, was in splendid condition. She had only just returned to service after a refit lasting some months, costing between £5,000 and £6,000. For most of the time since she was taken into service in 1838 she had been running to Cork, handled by a crew that seems to have varied in total somewhere between 16 and 19 officers and men.

During the refit Gardiner had the frustrating task of being a relief master for his company, the Bristol General Steam Navigation Company, and so when the *Queen* returned to service it was a welcome return for him too.

It is with her second voyage after the refit that we are concerned. She was being employed on relief duty. Bound for

Dublin she left Cumberland Basin in Bristol on Friday, 1 September, 1843. In addition to the crew she had at most 52 passengers all told.

Her cargo of 'British goods', carried in convenient containers like hampers and hogsheads or bundles and trusses, is listed below:

Holden & Co.	7 hogsheads, 6 tierces refined sugar
Hier & Co.	1 hogshead, 1 tierce ditto
J. & F. Savage	15 hogsheads, 1 tierce ditto
Lucas & Co.	1 crate glass
Lewis & Co.	10 hampers cheese
Webb & Co.	5 hampers ditto
Morgan & Co.	79 bars iron, 20 boxes tinplates
Arnold & Co.	7 trusses contents unknown
Withey & Co.	1 box linen
Thomas & Co.	100 spolees
Lunell & Co.	1 cask wine
Lediard & Co.	5 bags dye
Hughes & Co.	38 packs furniture
G. Downing	70 bundles wood hoops
Harford & Co.	75 rings wire
Nash & Co.	40 bundles iron, 34 boxes tinplates
Clarke & Co.	16 bales cotton

All was going well on the voyage. As the *Queen* steamed down the Bristol Channel it was a simply perfect September day. Capt. Gardiner wrote, ". . . we had the most beautiful weather that ever shone from the heavens.'

Off the South Pembrokeshire coast, having passed the St. Ann's Head lights, the *Queen* was taking a line between the island of Skokholm and the mainland about a mile and a half away. It was her captain's intention to continue then a course to take her through Broad Sound, a passage nearly two miles across between the islands of Skokholm and Skomer.

The course set by Capt. Gardiner was a fair weather one commonly taken by the Irish packet steamers. It had advantages; it relieved the tedium of the voyage for the passengers by giving them a view of the magnificent coastline; and by taking a more direct route it shortened the voyage. From the company's point of view it saved fuel.

There were, however, disadvantages to this course. And Capt. Gardiner was about to discover the treacherous side of the Pembrokeshire coast for himself. As he wrote:

'About twenty minutes past ten p.m., and very clear weather, as clear as day, we were abreast Milford lights, and steering a direct course for the Broad Sound, between Skokholm and Skomer, and as we were entering the sound it came on a dense fog, so much so that we could not see the ship's head.'

Only the captain could describe what happened next. In a letter written two days later, he said:

'I immediately put the ship's helm hard a-port, and brought her head S.S.E. to make the Milford lights, and then shape my course outside the island.'

In simple terms Capt. Gardiner had ordered a U-turn.

He continued:

'I gave my order to the engineer to slow the engines – quite slow. The orders were strictly obeyed. At the same time I sent Mr. Rees, the chief officer, to the engineer to fix his handles ready to stop or reverse her, as I might require – at this time going quite slow.

'Scarcely had these orders been given, before the look-out called out – "Hard a-port! A vessel right ahead!"'

But it was not a vessel; it was the island of Skokholm.

'We could not see what it was until we saw the breakers against the rocks.

'We reversed the engines, and she backed off, and we directed our course for Milford, thinking to save the ship.'

The Rev. S. D. Waddy, a Wesleyan minister from Bath, on his way to Dublin, saw matters in much the same light:

'The day was fine, and the night was particularly clear until we were passing between the islands of Skomer and Skokholm, near Milford Haven, when we were suddenly enveloped by a dense fog, which at once obscured the land previously in sight. As soon as this occurred the Captain checked the speed of the vessel, and turned round in hopes of discovering the Milford lights; in this attempt the vessel struck upon a rock close to the island of Skokholm.

'The shock was by no means severe . . . Considerable alarm was excited at the moment; but, from the very slow rate at which we were going when she struck, the apparently slight nature of the shock, and the ease with which she was got off, we were easily persuaded to believe that the vessel was not seriously injured, and that we were not in very imminent danger.

'Under this impression many of the female passengers did

not at once proceed to dress themselves, and some were not even awakened by the shock.

'A very few minutes, however, served to dispel any favourable impression which had been formed of our position. The vessel was evidently filling very fast, and there was no prospect of her continuing long above water.

'Just at this moment the scene was truly awful; the alarm and consternation of both passengers and crew, the ceaseless screaming of the steam whistle – some were praying – one man, frantic with fear, was blaspheming horribly.'

About a mile from where she struck, with, the captain judged, about ten feet of water in the hold, the *Queen* was fast settling forward by the head.

Waddy noted the engine had stopped, and now the *Queen* was drifting with the tide in deep water.

All seemed lost, and they were waiting for the inevitable.

Also lost, and also in terror was David Jenkins and his one man crew in the sloop *Hope*, a small vessel of 14 tons burthen.

They were in terror of being run down by the steamer, whose hideous screeching had come to them out of the fog.

The *Hope* had left Milford Haven that morning with a cargo of limestone. Running into fog she had become lost and was lying waiting for it to clear. As a local man David Jenkins knew the risks.

Hearing the *Queen's* whistle, Jenkins had set up a candle-lit lantern to give some warning however feeble of the *Hope's* presence.

And now, quite unexpectedly, Jenkins found himself cast in the role of rescuer, for his lantern light was seen from the *Queen*, now with a clear list to port to add to her troubles.

Capt. Gardiner hailed the *Hope* and, as she drew alongside, a passenger noticed that the top of her mast reached the top of the *Queen's* paddle-box.

No time was to be lost.

Waddy described the scene:

'The women (of whom there were about ten or twelve on board) were first embarked. One man stood in the shrouds of the *Hope* to whom the women were handed out of the steamer, and he then handed them down to another man on the deck.

'Several of them were in their night clothes, and without shoes. There was no time for them to dress after they had been informed of their danger. They were hurried off without time even to secure their watches and money . . .'

By the time the *Hope* was ready to push off, there was a fresh danger. In the process of sinking, the *Queen's* paddle-box was pressing down on the *Hope's* cat-head. It took a struggle to dislodge the *Hope*; and it was a great relief when she managed to push off to a safe distance to avoid being sucked down with the *Queen*. The crew, who were in the two ship's boats, stood off, waiting and watching hopelessly.

The *Hope*, which had been fully laden with limestone, now had the additional weight of the passengers on board, about fifty of them. She lay so low in the water her sides were, perhaps, only three inches above the surface. A single gust of wind could have swept in enough water to sink her.

Everyone was made to sit down, Waddy noted, save those who were needed to work the vessel and the four or five who were squeezed into the cabin.

Anchoring at a safe distance from the *Queen* which was drifting away, Jenkins saw to it that the *Hope* was made safer. In order to lighten her about two-thirds of the limestone was thrown overboard. And there she stood; Jenkins could not be persuaded to stir.

The crew, in the meantime, was forced to leave the *Queen* to her fate and seek out the *Hope* through the fog, guided to her by the shouts of the passengers and the feeble light of the lantern.

When all were together, it was time to take stock of the situation. A check was made. Almost at once they found there was one passenger missing. John Lary, an Irish 'pig-jobber', a man of about fifty, who walked with great difficulty with the aid of two sticks, was not with them.

Lary, a deck passenger, had gone down into the hold, it was suggested, to find himself a comfortable bed among the goods there. The other pig men knew him to be a very sound sleeper. Thus he had been overlooked when the officers had made their last-minute search by shouting down all the hatches.

Captain Gardiner on discovering this acted at once. He took the ship's boats and they went back to the *Queen* to look for Lary.

Waddy thought they were away more than an hour, rowing fruitlessly about. And during this time, to alleviate the anxiety of those on board the *Hope*, a musket was fired at intervals with the idea of keeping the ship's crew aware of their position, and to attract the attention of any other vessel that might happen to be within earshot.

When the boats came back at last, they were moored to the *Hope*. And thus the rest of the night was spent, with everyone silent, listening and waiting for the dawn, with all the candles dowsed save one and the occasional crack of the musket.

When morning came the fog was still about. No land could be seen; but waves could be heard distinctly, breaking against the rocks of the shore.

About 8 o'clock, Capt. Gardiner, taking one of the ship's boats and four men with him, made his move. His plan was to go as close to the coast as possible, and by going among them, follow the line of the breakers until he could find the entrance into Milford Haven itself. It was a hazardous enterprise.

Those left behind decided to relieve their anxieties by action also. They moved in a somewhat desultory fashion in the direction of Milford Haven; desultory because the fog persisted and some were fearful that if they moved too far they might be missed by the rescuers.

It was the turning tide that changed their minds, for, since they could make little headway against it, they resolved to wait until the tide changed again.

They had been without food since the previous evening. "Our stock of provisions,' wrote Waddy, 'consisted of two loaves of bread, some raw bacon and a little butter. Some bread and butter had been given to the women and children; and the rest of the bread and the raw bacon . . . was divided among the men who had worked the hardest . . .'

The tide, Waddy noticed, changed about 2 o'clock, and it brought with it a gleam of sun, which broke through the fog for about twenty minutes. This gave them enough time to organise the remaining ship's boat to take the *Hope* in tow, and set off for the Haven with St. Ann's Head itself now in view.

There were large oars and small oars, and the passengers did what they could with them. And thus they proceeded.

Capt. Gardiner's plan worked. His ship's boat found its way to Milford (that is the place within the great Haven). There he found the Trinity House steamer was being repaired and could not put to sea. However, the commander of the *Skylark*, a revenue cutter, on being told of the situation, put to sea at once.

The *Skylark*, attended by the Lloyd's agent's boat, came across the *Hope* as she was struggling to enter the Haven, and in danger of being forced by the sea onto the headland rocks.

The ordeal was over.

Waddy again:

'The commander of the cutter (whose name, I believe, was Johnson) treated us with the greatest kindness. The sudden sense of security, and the heartiness with which he offered us anything in his vessel, overcame the feelings of many who, up to this time, had remained apparently unmoved, and both men and women wept.'

Now that their lives were safe, the passengers became aware of what they had lost. Waddy counted the cost:

'Some were without hats, some were without shoes, and some almost without clothing of any kind but their night-dresses, and almost all without money; several, among whom was a clergyman of respectability, were passed on to Waterford, under a magistrate's order, as totally destitute. We all, with perhaps one single exception, lost everything but the clothes we happened to have on.

'I should have saved my mackintosh, but when the *Queen* was going down, a gentleman who saw it in my hand advised me not to encumber myself with it, and I laid it down.

'There were some cases of loss truly heart-rending. One man lost £2,000 in sovereigns, the entire savings of twenty years; he had written to his father to purchase him a small farm in the north of Ireland; he was going over with his money to pay for it, and with his wife and child to settle on his native spot for the rest of his life. Many others were left equally destitute, although their losses were much less in amount.'

The passengers and crew were treated most hospitably by the people of Milford. On the day following their rescue, a Sunday, they all went to church 'to return thanks for their providential deliverance.' And that day Capt. Gardiner penned a letter to the owners of the *Queen* giving his account of the events; not surprisingly, in his state of mind, leaving out important parts of the story.

Two passengers wrote accounts praising Capt. Gardiner, '. . . coolness and courage . . . last man to leave . . . no want of skill . . . kindness and attention . . .'

*

But, of course, the matter did not rest there. Once the loss of the *Queen* had become public knowledge questions were bound to be asked.

An editorial in the Bristol Mirror gave the background to the operations of the packet steamer companies. It stated that there had been heavy investment in the steam navigation boom, resulting in fierce competition, which had in turn led to charges and profits being below their proper level. Very few companies were flourishing, it continued, the implication being, as a result, the steamer companies were anxious to reduce expenditure and cut costs.

Why, the paper asked, did not the captain cast anchor and wait for the fog to clear?

In the Times 'Viator' drew attention to the similarity between the loss of the *Queen* and that of the *Pegasus*, the Leith to Hull steamer, which going inside the 'Fern' Islands, had, only a month before, struck a sunken rock with great loss of life.

After pointing out that both the ships had returned to deep water after being holed, 'Viator' continued the parallel with regard to what seems to have been their utter neglect of the hand-lead, the "seaman's safeguard" he called it. For the *Queen* in her predicament, 'Surely the chief, if not the only, means of safety, was to "feel the way with the lead." No doubt,' concluded 'Viator', 'we shall be told that the captain is a person of unquestioned skill and experience.'

William Rees, chief officer of the *Queen*, in his reply also printed in The Times, refuted 'Viator's assertions:

'I appeal to any nautical man acquainted with the coast of Pembrokeshire, particularly in the locality of Skokholm and Skomer Islands, whether the lead would be of the least effective service where the general average of water runs from 14 to 16 fathoms quite close to the rocks; indeed, in most places, there is scarcely any difference in the depth of water close along shore and in the fairway . . .'

The point, in general terms, was well made. However, as a matter of fact, Denham's chart, the very best available at the time, would suggest extreme caution rounding the north-east corner of Skokholm in fog. An area roughly semi-circular in shape, about 1 cable in diameter, and containing The Stack, is given on the chart a depth of no more than one fathom with the possibility of submerged rocks, whereas the *Queen* required roughly two fathoms of clear water.

If Captain Gardiner's judgment over the way he reacted to the fog was called into question, there remained strong points carried in the newspapers criticising the policies of the steam packet companies which put their captains in an exposed position, particularly when weather conditions were adverse.

For example, the Bristol Mercury called 'the attention of the public and especially the proprietors of these large transit boats, to the folly and sin of risking property and life for the mere accommodation of shortening a long voyage by two or three hours. The facility of taking short cuts, by going nearer shore than a sailing vessel would ever venture, has already made steam navigation more perilous than the old method. . .' This point and others were made in newspapers from The Times in London to the Welshman published in Carmarthen.

In the Welshman was carried a letter from 'A Frequent Voyager By The Company's Ships'. It made some stinging points.

Stating that ten of the Bristol General Steam Navigation Company's ships made weekly voyages to Ilfracombe, West Wales and Southern Ireland; the writer went on to note that four of their finest ships had been lost within the last five years, and calculated that if things continued in this way the company would have lost them all in twelve and a half years. Furthermore, he was convinced that it was the desire to save coal that led to steamers hugging the coastline, a policy that led to disaster.

His final point: the *Queen* had boats capable of holding the ship's crew only, so that the whole of the passengers must have perished, but for the interposition of God. 'When it is so easy to have boats capable of holding every person on board even in heavy weather, what shall be said of the criminal penuriousness of a set of men who can continue to set their ships to sea, after so many and severe warnings, with two small skiffs and but 2 (or 3) life preservers on deck.'

Writing from London to The Times, Mr. Thomas Motley pressed the value of the cork waistcoat as a life preserver at sea. And in its pockets, he thought, might be secreted a telescopic handle, from which could be flown a streamer or flag, and a boatswain's whistle. The whole thing would cost from 15 to 30 shillings.

The Times published a wide-ranging letter from Mr. J. E. Fitzgerald, who seems to have had much more than a passing knowledge of the Bristol Channel and its shipping, and who claims to have been out in the Channel on the night the *Queen* went down and the night before.

His letter is critical of the way the *Queen* was being navigated; finding it hard to understand how, after passing the Milford lights with a clear view, they should have got so far out of their reckoning in so short a time, as to be so disastrously close to Skokholm on entering Broad Sound. Basing his conclusion on information provided by Capt. Gardiner's letter to the owners, which was published in the press, Fitzgerald was of the opinion that the *Queen* must have overrun her reckoning, must have actually passed through the Sound, and have run ashore on the way back. He doubted that the *Queen* could have run into a dense bank of fog without some intimation that there was fog coming on. And, given the conditions existing at the time, Fitzgerald, like other critics, felt sure that the ship should have been brought to anchor instantly.

With regard to the policy of the companies, which allowed their steamers to sail close to the coastline in fair weather, he was forthright. 'It does appear a monstrous absurdity that there are numbers of old craft, scarcely seaworthy, navigated in safety for 30 or 40 years in all weathers about the Channel, and that a noble ship like the *Queen* should be lost on a perfectly calm night. The reason, Sir, is this – that the steamers run close to all dangers for the sake of making short cuts, and saving an hour on the passage.'

As for the wider implications, Fitzgerald was concerned that the *Queen* should have made the same error that had been pointed out at the time of the wreck of the *Pegasus*, by moving into deep water when holed. He suggested that officers responsible for steam packets should be held accountable for their actions just as naval officers were in a court martial.

He went on to make the point that passengers travelling on railroads had laws and inspectors to protect them, but those on sea, exposed as they were to much greater danger, enjoyed no such protection from the law.

Fitzgerald, in conclusion, stated firmly, 'The public have no mode of insisting on the caution and attention of those in command of public conveyances by sea, except by diligently scrutinising the causes of an accident, and visiting the authors with their displeasure.' He ends with fairness. 'I do not mean to charge anyone with neglect in the present instance, I only say that it is a case that demands investigation.'

This public reaction to the disaster of the *Queen* raised many questions to be considered in the future.

But for the moment there was honour to be paid to the hero, David Jenkins, master of the *Hope*. A certificate was presented to him.

'We the undersigned Captain, crew, and passengers on board the packet called the *Queen*, sailing from Bristol to Dublin, on Friday, 1st September, 1843, do hereby certify that David Jenkins of the sloop *Hope*, did, at the risk of his own life and the loss of his vessel, about twenty minutes past eleven o'clock at night on the said 1st September, rescue from destruction the whole of the passengers and crew, with the exception of one, in all sixty-seven souls; and we beg thus publicly to declare that to the courage, steadiness, and kindness of Captain Jenkins we attribute, under God, our miraculous preservation.

Anne Caroline La Touche, Fanny La Touche, Anne C. La Touche, E. L. La Touche, Anne Norton Smith, Robert F. Ellis, J. Barker, E. S. Barker, Dennis George, Robert Handcock, D.D., Jane Handcock, Martha Handcock, Thomas Downes, M. C. Downes, C. C. Gardiner, commander, George Rowles, second mate, Thomas Lloyd, steward.'

In Dublin a subscription was raised on behalf Capt. Jenkins and his crewman. In Bristol Mr. R. W. Burton of 2, Saville Place suggested a similar effort.

Apart from those already mentioned, the names of a few other passengers are known: a Mr. Rogers and a Mr. Hare, both of Bristol; The Rev. Mr. Bredan and a Mr. Crosbie. Mrs. La Touche was the wife of John La Touche of Marley, the Rev. Thomas Handcock was of St. Thomas' Dublin and Mr. Barker was a solicitor of Bristol. George Rowles, the second mate, we have met before, as mate on the *Killarney*.

As a postscript, the sea offered up its flotsam within hours, amongst it two trunks containing jewellery. Two days later, however, a little dog was found alive floating about on a piece of the wreckage in St. Brides Bay. It belonged to Capt. Gardiner and was restored to him.

6. Matters Arising

It was a time of remarkable enterprise when all these events took place; when great commercial risks were taken; when enterprises often grew or failed spectacularly; when problems, that in days before would have been managed by local laws, grew to a scale that needed Parliamentary legislation.

The dilemma facing government was to balance enterprise and regulation. The desire of Parliament was to show some activity, but the drawing up of safety regulations was a matter of fiendish difficulty. Regulations to be effective had to be both enforceable by the authorities, and acceptable to the owners who took the risks, had to pay the costs, and had to be convinced that the regulations were workable.

Five ships sunk in twelve years out of an operating fleet of about a dozen, this was a disastrous run for the Bristol steam packet company. These disasters had their place in the concern of the nation at large about shipwrecks. While everyone was touched at the heroism of Grace Darling at the time of the loss of the *Forfarshire*, people were appalled at the numbers of ships wrecked and the great loss of life.

What was done?

That Parliament reflected the general concern shown by the public about the great loss of life at sea is to be seen in the Parlimentary Select Committees of 1836 and 1843. They made a number of recommendations and paved the way for the Merchant Shipping Act of 1850, which gave legislative force to many of them. Not only did the Act make a start in dealing with particular problems, but it made a beginning in the organising of the shipping industry under one government department – the Board of Trade.

Looking at the Bristol company's shipwrecks, and taking all this into account, it is worth looking at the causes and see how they were remedied.

It seems likely that the company had second thoughts about

leaving the choice of course to the discretion of its captains. The *Albion* and *Queen* had both been lost in taking the cost-cutting, scenic route among Skomer and Skokholm Islands. That was simply bad practice which could be corrected easily.

In the case of the *City of Bristol* and the *Queen*, where navigational skill was in question, the Merchant Shipping Act of 1850 provided for the compulsory examination of masters and mates, where the successful earned a certificate. And incidentally from 1862 Irish packets among others had to carry at least one certificated engineer. This upgrading of ships' officers was a great step in improving their quality.

As to ships' boats, apart from their inadequate capacity, like the two on the *Queen*, for example, which on the evidence of a passenger were capable of carrying only about 20 people between them, often in emergency they were swamped through being badly handled.

When regulations for boats carried on sea-going passenger steamships were introduced in the early 1850's, they contained a scale for ships' boats to be provided according to tonnage, not according to the maximum number of people on board. So that a passenger steamer like the *Queen*, for example, under the regulations of the Merchant Shipping Act of 1854, would have carried in simplest terms 3 or 4 boats; or, as the scale laid down, one 16ft. boat and a 22ft. one, and a 22ft. launch or, instead of the launch, two 22ft. boats or two paddlebox boats.

However, the *Titanic* disaster of 1912 exposed to the world the gross inadequacy of providing lifesaving equipment on a basis other than per person on board. It transpired that there were only 1,178 boat spaces for 2,224 people on board. At the same time the reluctance of some passengers on the *Titanic* to get into the lifeboats brought to the fore the need for lifeboat drill.

The action of the Government in the particular case of the *Killarney* is interesting. The loss of the *Killarney* had created a sensation. Press reports, unique pictures in the papers, a book written by a survivor and the fact some of those involved in the tragedy had influential connections, all these conspired to keep the public interest alive.

The findings of the jury complaining about the number of pigs carried on the *Killarney* were brought to the attention of the "proper authorities", that is the Government in the House of Commons, by Lord Ebrington. The President of the Board of

Trade undertook to look into the matter. And so he did.

The Admiralty offered no help in the projected inquiry; they could not spare the officers. So help was sought from Lord Glenelg at the Colonial Office. He instructed the Government Emigration Office based at 2, Middle Scotland Yard, which arranged for the Emigration Officers stationed at the relevant Irish ports to undertake the task of making inquiries according to a clear government brief.

The resulting reports were to be sent to Office of the Committee of the Privy Council for Trade, in short the Board of Trade, together 'with any suggestions to satisfy the public mind, and with a view to the introduction of some legislative measure on the subject.'

Thus the Government inquiry received information from officials on the spot.

Lieut. Edward Miller, R.N., from Belfast, prefaced his observations with the reminder that the Irish trade in pigs and horned cattle was important, and that rapid transit by steam-boat was much to be desired.

He thought that a cargo of pigs on deck should be confined within strong barricades, leaving a clear gangway on each side for sailors to go about their business. The reports from Cork and Dublin said much the same thing.

With regard to the restriction of numbers, he thought that it was difficult to lay down rules and suggested officers be appointed to regulate the carriage of animals according to the prevailing circumstances.

From Dublin came the more practical view that, confined amidships within secure boards, pigs so carried would be safe, and there would be no need to limit according to numbers or weight.

In contrast, Lieut. Charles Friend, R.N., from Cork, favoured a more mathematical approach and gave the following table:

1 pig per ton register
1 sheep or calf = 1 pig
1 horned cattle = 2 pigs

The other important part of the inquiry was to discover the extent of the problem of deck cargoes of pigs in winter.

The time for pigs and cattle in general to be considered as living creatures with their own need of protection by the law, and not as a deck cargo which like timber might become dangerous in heavy sea, lay far into the future.

Londonderry had heard of no problems with pigs. From Dublin Lieut. T. E. Hodder, R.N., said no instance was known to him of pigs being thrown overboard from Dublin ships. Friend at Cork said he had heard of only one occasion there despite ships sailing through the winter in all weathers.

The report from Cork presented evidence obtained from steamer captains. Mr. Parker of the *Victory*, 250 tons, said once in twelve years he had been forced in tremendous seas to jettison pigs. He had always used his own discretion and taken 600 pigs in summer and 500 in winter; in exceptional conditions they might be reduced to 250.

Mr. Pile of the *Ocean*, 300 tons, who in nearly twelve years had never thrown a deck cargo overboard, considered 700 pigs, 500 of them on deck, a safe cargo.

Much the same was said by Mr. Hyde of the *City of Bristol*.

Mr. Beale, managing agent of the St. George Packet Company, which had a vested interest in the pig trade, made two telling points, one general and one particular. He claimed that since the companies in the trade did not insure their vessels they had a decided interest in their safety. Moreover, if the *Killarney* had not been mechanically disabled, he believed the pigs would not have had to be thrown overboard.

And here it seems the matter rested. The reports were printed by order of the House of Commons on 18 June, 1838, that is six months after the disaster.

After a similar delay, allowing him time to come to terms with his terrible experience on the *Killarney*, Doctor Spolasco moved on.

For Baron Spolasco, M.D., M.R.C.S., K.O.M.T., C.L.D'H., the world was a stage.

Where a stylish entrance was needed, he was known to make his appearance 'in a carriage drawn by four horses, with postillions, hired to make a sensation.'

In dress 'the pink of fashion', he was, it seems, equally ready to dress and act the part of a mountebank, when required.

He made his entrances and exits, and for him scene shifting meant moving on.

'In taking leave of the Citizens of Limerick, being called away by other duties, Doctor Spolasco feels confident that he carries with him the blessings of thousands, who, when pronounced incurable by the most eminent practitioners, had

BARON SPOLASCO. M.D.
& M.R.C.S.—K.O.M.T.& C.L.D'.H.

18. *Portrait of Baron Spolasco*: lithograph, Jn. Unkles, 1838, from a painting by Signor Fabroni (by kind permission of the Bristol Reference Library). 'In dress "the pink of fashion" . . .'

recourse to him, and in most instances, under Divine Providence, were restored to perfect health.'
After Limerick it was to Cork.
'The Baron being at present on a tour through the principal Cities of Europe, takes leave to announce his arrival in Cork . . .'
Newspapers, pamphlets and broadsheets were his means of

self-advertisement. He claimed his treatments to have been 'peculiarly successful' in a long list of 'diseases'; among them Small Pox and Flatulency, Costiveness and Worms, Want of Appetite, Eructations and Leprosy, Frightful Dreams and Dropsy, Fistula and Gleet, Insanity and Foul Breath; nothing, it seems defied his skill.

'In Surgical Operations and Bone-Setting the Baron stands unrivalled . . .'. His "talicotian operation", by which he claimed to have given a Limerick man a new nose, was undoubtedly a form of plastic surgery. Midwifery was another of his skills.

Then there were his patent medicines; Balm of Spolasco for 'the enfeebled and debilitated': Antiphroditic for 'Married Females of a pure and affectionate disposition . . .': Poor Man's Treasure or Celebrated Ointment of Venice: and tooth powder, and treatments for the skin and hair.

As for his 'Life Preservers', since their introduction 'into boarding schools, manufactories, coal, and lead mines &., thousands have been annually preserved from internal disorders. . . . They are an infallible cure for some, and an undoubted remedy for many internal disorders, to which all are more or less liable. They are also calculated to prevent sea-sickness. . . . These pills are so celebrated that they supersede the use of other medicines both by sea and land. . . . They should be taken by everyone, old and young, male and female, twice a week.'

The prescription, it was claimed, purified the blood and renovated the system. 'Three or four of box, No.1, on going to bed, with the addition of two or three of box, No.2, in the morning after a debauch, will entirely counteract all the ill effects experienced from it.'

Yet there were still the 'Vegetable Patent Pills', which Spolasco said the Admiralty had ruled sailors were to take twice a week 'to sweeten and purify the system – seeing that they prevent coughs, colds, and all contagious diseases' – no mention of sea-sickness here. They were 'also much used by the Army, Constabulary, and in Boarding-schools, Manufactories &..'

With his usual timing, Spolasco left Cork for Bristol to consult, as he said, with the agent of a very High Personage.

And then the *Killarney*.

Spolasco bounced back from the trauma of the shipwreck, and his own personal tragedy. His appearance before the jury

> Teeth, price 5s., to be had at the above Establishment.
>
> "SUNT MILLE MALA, SUNT ETIAM REMEDIA."
>
> MOST IMPORTANT TO ALL CLASSES OF SOCIETY!
>
> THE Celebrated BARON SPOLASCO, M.D., A.B., M.R.C.S., K.O.M.T., and C.L.D'H., recently arrived from the Continent, being on a tour through the principal cities of Europe, has just arrived in Bristol, and may be consulted at his residence, 5, COLLEGE-GREEN, from 10 o'clock in the Morning until 6 in the Afternoon, relative to all the Diseases incidental to human nature.
>
> The Baron is a Licentiate Physician and Member of the Royal College of Surgeons. He was a *perpetual* pupil of the late celebrated BARON DUPUYTREN, of the Hotel-Dieu, Paris, and studied the various branches of his profession in the Universities of Paris, Berlin, Leyden, London, Edinburgh, Glasgow, and Dublin.
>
> He is consulted, in cases of difficulty and danger, by Physicians and Surgeons in all parts of the world!!!
>
> Certificates of the Baron's wonderful cures may be seen by reference to his pamphlets.
>
> The Baron's system of treating diseases is altogether peculiar to himself, and so successful that it has scarcely in any instance been known to fail.
>
> In consequence of the number of sufferers who daily crowd round Baron Spolasco's consulting rooms, he has found it necessary, in order to save his valuable time, to charge an admission fee of 5s., which admission fee, if the patient be poor, will be received as a consideration for the Baron's advice: the wealthy will, of course, have to pay the usual fee of a guinea.
>
> Those who are anxious to consult Baron Spolasco would do well to make *immediate application*, as his stay in Bristol, must, necessarily, be very limited.
>
> A second edition of Dr. Spolasco's interesting NARRATIVE of the DISASTROUS WRECK of the Steamer, *Killarney*, has just been published, and may be had of all booksellers.

19. Baron Spolasco: advertisement, Bristol Gazette (by kind permission of the Bristol Reference Library). Within six months of the *Killarney* disaster Spolasco had set up consulting rooms in Bristol at 5, College Green.

summoned to his room was dramatic. But soon the old drive was back and he was in Cork writing and publishing his book about the shipwreck. He organised the printer and lithographer to do the work for the printing and paper only. And Signor Fabroni, the artist, painted Spolasco's portrait for nothing.

The book showed Spolasco had a talent for writing. His sense of drama allowed the story to be well told. However, the quack was not far away. Space at the end of the book was not wasted. It was hurriedly crammed with certificates of cures and other dubious material used in his advertising. He did not miss the opportunity to announce that he was still in business.

'Baron Spolasco has found it necessary, in order to protect himself from unnecessary intrusion, to charge an admission of five shillings, which admission fee, if the person be poor, will be received as a consideration for the Baron's advice. The wealthy will, of course, have to pay the usual fee of a guinea. The Baron being now convalescent has resumed his professional avocations and may be consulted at his residence, 4, King Street.'

Within six months of the disaster he was set up on College Green in Bristol advertising his presence in the Bristol papers. On his billheads came to be printed, by way of recommendation, that he was a survivor of the *Killarney* shipwreck.

Eventually he turned up in New York, 'the brims of the hat curling like the top of a Corinthian column', but, as they say, that is another story.

Glossary

bastard sugar an impure coarse brown sugar, made from the refuse syrup of previous boilings.
binnacle the housing for the mariner's compass etc.
bower anchor one of the two anchors which are carried on either side of a ship's bows.
cable a measure of distance at sea of 200 yards or 100 fathoms.
cat-head a heavy piece of curved timber projecting from the bow of a ship on each side for the purpose of holding anchors.
capillaire a syrup made of maidenhair fern; syrup flavoured with orange-flower water; here it is used whimsically, the poet has an eye for the young ladies, they add pleasure to the feast.
fathom a measure of depth or distance at sea of 6 feet or 1·8256 metres.
hogshead a large cask usually of about 50 imperial gallons.
nautical or **sea mile** a measure of 6080 feet; a rule of thumb measurement would be 10 sea miles to roughly $11\frac{1}{2}$ land or statutory miles.
packet a vessel plying at regular intervals between two ports for the conveyance of mails also of goods and passengers: but came in time to refer to such a vessel whether mail was carried or not.
puncheon a large cask holding 72–120 gallons.
quadrant inter alia, a metal frame, shaped as the quadrant or sector of a circle that is fixed to the rudder head or stock and to which the steering ropes or chains are attached.
shrouds rigging giving lateral support to the mast, as opposed to fore and aft support.
spole (obsolete or dialect) a spool.
tabinet or **tabbinett** a watered fabric of silk and wool resembling poplin: chiefly associated with Ireland.
taffrail the rail at the very back of the ship.
Taliacotrian as in Taliacotrian operation, a plastic operation described by Tagliacozzi, a surgeon of Bologna (1546–99), for restoration of the nose by means of tissue taken from another part.

tierce a medium-sized cask containing a certain quantity which varies with goods; especially provisions.

tonnage tons burthen a measurement intended to indicate the cargo carrying capacity of a ship on which dues had to be paid.

  gross tonnage used by shipbuilders to calculate the cost of building a ship per ton.

  registered tonnage a measurement used by the authorities concerned to charge dues. The various systems of measuring tonnage pass the wisdom of Solomon.

wharfinger the owner or keeper of a wharf.

Bibliography

Newspapers published in Bristol, Cork, London, Bath, Swansea and Carmarthen.
Baron Spolasco. *Narrative of the wreck of the steamer Killarney*, (Cork, 1838).
House of Commons Parliamentary Papers. *Select Committee on the Milford Haven Communications, 1827* and *Correspondence relative to the Loss of the Killarney Steamer &c., 1838.* (Chadwyck-Healey microfiche).
Farr, Grahame E.: *Records of Bristol Ships 1800-1838 (Vessels over 150 tons)*, (B.R.S. vol.XV): and *Chepstow Ships*, (The Chepstow Society, 1954)
Bristol Presentments.
Port of Milford Register of Ships from 1827.
Admiralty Charts, especially the relevant ones based on the surveys of Lieut. H.M. Denham, R.N..
The Ordnance Survey.
Directories: Mathews's for Bristol.
        Pigot's for South Wales.
Parish registers, various.
Bristol Corporation Assize of Bread.
Parish of Castle Precincts Consolidated Rate Book 1823/4.
Westbury on Trym Poor House Order Book 1822/3.
Gentleman's Magazine, 1858.
Manuscript:PRO: Crew Lists BT/98/90+.
        NLW: Llwyngwair Mss. 16995.
           Colt Hoare, Journey 179? Mss. 16988-9.
        Haverfordwest RO:Trearched Papers,
           HDX/467/10.
Frolic ballad, collected by Harry Griffiths of Haverfordwest and communicated to the Pembrokeshire County Guardian by Mr. J. Cornock of Hakin, 15th. May, 1947.

Blackburn, Graham. *Illustrated Dictionary of Nautical Terms*, (David and Charles, Newton Abbot, 1981).

Bull, J.W. *An Introduction to Safety at Sea*, (Brown, Son & Ferguson, 1981).
Course, Capt. A. G. *Dictionary of Nautical Terms*, (ARCO, 1962) and *The Merchant Navy: A Social History*, (London, 1963).
Davies, Peter B. S. *Deadly Perils*, (Merrivale, 1992).
Farr, Grahame E. *West Country Passenger Steamers*, (T. Stephenson and Son, Prescot, Lancs., 2nd. edn., 1967), and *Bristol Shipbuilding in the Nineteenth Century*, (Bristol Hist. Assoc., 1971); and *Shipbuilding in the Port of Bristol*, (National Maritime Museum, Martime Monographs and Reports No. 27, 1977).
George, Barbara. *Pembrokeshire Sea-Trading Before 1900*, (London, 1964).
Gill, Jennifer. *The Bristol Scene, views of Bristol by Bristol artists...*, (Redcliffe Press, 1986).
Greenacre, Francis. *Marine Artists of Bristol: Nicholas Pocock: Joseph Walter*, (City of Bristol Museum and Art Gallery, 1982).
Hall, Samuel Carter. *Retrospect of a Long Life:* 2 vols. (London, 1882).
Hill, John C. G. *Shipshape and Bristol Fashion*, (Redcliffe Press, 1983).
Hope, Ronald. *A New History of British Shipping*, (John Murray, 1990).
Jackson, Gordon. *The History and Archaeology of Ports*, (World's Work, 1983).
Kemp, Peter. *The Oxford Companion to Ships and the Sea*, (O.U.P., 1976).
Latimer, John. *The Annals of Bristol in the Nineteenth Century*, (Bristol, 1887).
Magrath, Patrick. *The Merchant Venturers of Bristol*, (Society of Merchant Venturers, 1975), and ed. *Bristol in the 18th. Century*, (David and Charles, 1972).
Macmillan, Daniel. *Treatise on the Law of Merchant Shipping*, (2nd. ed. Maxwell, 1875).
McKay, Wing. Cdr. K. D. *A Vision of Greatness: the History of Milford, 1790–1990*, (Brace Harvatt Associates, 1989).
Parsons, R. M. *A History of the Bristol Steam Navigation Company*, (Articles in Sea Breezes, vol. 55, 1981).
Scott's Shipbuilding and Engineering Ltd. *Two Hundred and Fifty Years of Shipbuilding*, (Privately, 1961).
Shields, John. *Clyde built: a history of Shipbuilding on the River Clyde*, (Glasgow, Maclennan, 1949).

Smart, J. F. *The Steam Packet*, (Wansbrough and Saunders, Bristol, 1823).

Torrens, Hugh. *The Winwood Family*, (Article in BIAS Journal, 1980).

Vaughan, W.E. (ed.). *A New History of Ireland*, vol.v, (Clarendon Press, 1989).

Waters, Brian. *The Bristol Channel*, (Dent, 1955).

Waters, Ivor. *Chepstow Packets*, (Moss Rose Press, Chepstow, 1983).

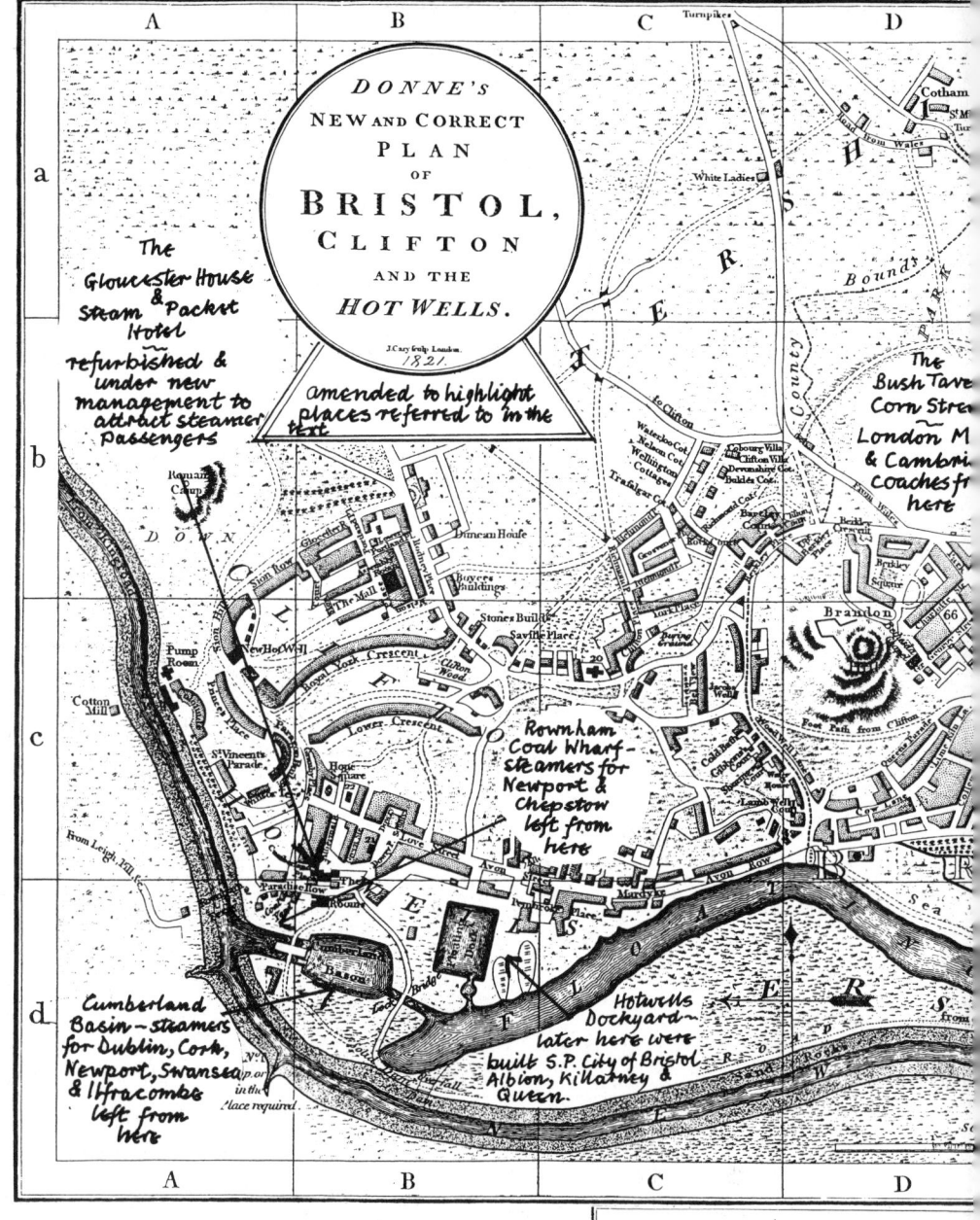

Map 8: Bristol c. 1820: **Donne's New and Correct Plan of Bristol, Clifton and the Hotwells**: amended to highlight places referred to in the text.